Mind Over Matter

MIND OVER MATTER

A scientist's view of the paranormal

KIT PEDLER

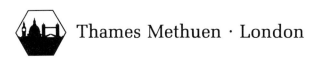 Thames Methuen · London

For Cherry

First published 1981 in Great Britain
by Eyre Methuen Ltd
11 New Fetter Lane, London EC4P 4EE
in association with
Thames Television International Ltd
149 Tottenham Court Road, London W1P 9LL

ISBN 0 423 00120 5

Printed in Great Britain
by Fakenham Press Limited
Fakenham, Norfolk

Contents

6

Acknowledgements

This book is the result of a very happy association with many friends at Thames Television. So, my grateful thanks to:

Richard Mervyn for his expert and imaginative production of the television series.

Tony Bastable for initiating the whole project and co-presenting the series.

Ian Martin and Diana Potter for their enthusiastic support and encouragement.

Frederica Lord for her knowledgeable and copious research.

Nic Jones of Thames Publishing for editorial care, creative criticism and great encouragement.

Sally Barnsley for holding it all together so splendidly.

The location film crew: Frank Hodge, David Engelman, George Thomas, Roger Stamp and Allan McMillan, for their friendly and often ferocious criticism.

Brian Inglis for reading and criticising the manuscript.

Eleanor O'Keefe for much useful bibliographic information.

Bernard Allum for illustrating the series so excellently and designing the book cover.

The many scientists who contributed so many fascinating ideas and who gave of their time so generously.

Siobhan Phelan for photography.

Pauline Mason for making sense of my hideous handwriting.

Thanks also to the following for photographs:

Keystone (1, 3, 47), Lotte Meitner Graf (2), BBC HPL (9), Camera Press (35, 36), *Sunday Times* (Frank Hermann) (39), Audio Ltd (G. Blundell) (48).

Illustrations

Introduction

Mind Over Matter is about unusual connections between the human mind and the outside world. It stems from the research, the voyage of discovery through the 'new' physics, which I embarked upon for the Thames Television series of the same name.

Most connections between the mind and the outside world are part of everyday experience. Our eyes take in the beauties of the universe for our mind to delight in, our hands sense the coolness of the grass, and we can effortlessly enjoy the scent of roses in the evening.

But some people claim to have entirely different connections with the world around them. Some believe that they can see directly into the future, or discover what someone else is experiencing miles away. Because the abilities claimed cannot involve any of the ordinary senses, they are called 'extra-sensory', and since they also involve a kind of perception, they are sometimes called 'extra-sensory-perception'.

Others call the study of these abilities 'parapsychology', but this sounds to me more like a study of mental illness, so I shall not be using the term. Neither shall I be using the word 'psychic', since this implies an act of belief in something untestable. Sometimes the overall name 'psi' is used, but this again has no clear meaning, and I shall use the term 'paranormal', which does have meaning since it means *alongside* the normal. I want to define very clearly indeed what I do mean by this word.

If a film is made of someone bending a teaspoon apparently by stroking it with a finger, the film could be a record of someone bending it quite normally. Just by looking at the film alone, I cannot *ever* decide whether the spoon was bent normally or paranormally, since I know film can be faked.

If, on the other hand, another person shows that a subject can bend a spoon when all other normal causes have been positively ruled out, I can conclude that the metal *was* bent paranormally; that is to say, the bending occurred because of some influence which had nothing to do with normal physical processes – rather than, for example, that the bending occurred because the spoon bender heated it with a blow torch or secretly bent it by hand pressure.

Again, if someone else claims to predict events before they occur, then that person could be normally gullible, normally mistaken or even a normal liar. Yet an investigator may show that some future events can be accurately predicted by some people when gullibility, mistakes and fraud have all been positively ruled out. Then I call those predictions paranormal, since I would have to admit either that there are people who can look into the future paranormally, or that time itself is not the one-way, irreversible flow that we take for granted when we try to think about it.

When someone makes such a claim without ruling out all normal causes, this is an ordinary story or anecdote. The anecdote can be true or false or indeterminate. Anecdotal evidence can be true or false. The problem is deciding which. Obviously, if a friend tells us something (gives us 'anecdotal evidence') of an event which has just happened, we tend to believe him, because there is no reason why we should do otherwise. If he says, 'I've just eaten breakfast,' we accept that he has. But in the field of the paranormal, anecdotal evidence by itself is not alone enough to provide conclusive information. We have to create different rules for deciding whether an event is normal or paranormal.

It is for this reason that I have opened the book with a short look at the ground rules of evidence, the characteristics of an open mind, and what makes an experiment good or bad – so that you can make your own judgement for yourself. I have always distrusted 'experts' and 'specialists' who try to exclude 'laymen'. There was never anything difficult about science: it was only made so by some scientists, and I hope this section will help turn you into an investigator of the paranormal who is every bit as good as anyone else who claims special knowledge or skills in this area.

The whole field of the paranormal had, until recently, an uneasy, rather unhealthy ring to it. The image was of rotund old ladies sitting over tea and rock cakes playing rather sinister games with a ouija board, and there are stories of mediums and ectoplasm, butter muslin and ghostly trumpets floating in the semi-darkness of Victorian parlours.

Two factors changed my whole attitude to the subject. The first was that I discovered an immense body of good, hard, experimental evidence on the subject, often carried out by Nobel Laureates or others who had already proved themselves to be excellent in other fields of science.

The second was that I discovered that the science of physics itself had moved sharply towards a view of the universe which not only tends to validate the paranormal as a genuine reality but also shows the real fabric of things to be so strange, mysterious and fascinating that any well brought-up science fiction writer would give up in sheer despair. This second point was an enormous surprise to me. As a doctor and biological scientist, I had lived in various experimental laboratories since the age of eighteen and had become accustomed to the idea that nature was a process which was tidy and explicable if only one took it to bits for long enough and in enough detail.

Scientists who try to take nature to bits in this way and claim in the end that they will understand the whole of nature because they understand all of its parts are called 'reductionists'. Scientists who have taken nature to bits and then claim that their study of the parts reveals a whole which is greater than the sum of the parts are called 'holists'.

So for almost twenty years I occupied my research time as a happy biological reductionist believing that my painstaking research would eventually reveal ultimate truths. Then I began to read the new physics. The experience was shattering.

As a biologist I had imagined the physicists to be cool, clear, unemotional men and women who looked down on nature from a clinical, detached viewpoint – people who reduced a sunset to wavelengths and frequencies, and observers who shredded the complex of the universe into rigid and formal elements.

My error was enormous. I began to study the works of people with legendary names: Einstein, Bohr, Schrödinger and Dirac. I found that here were not clinical and detached men, but poetic and religious ones who imagined such unfamiliar immensities as to make what I have referred to as the 'paranormal' almost pedestrian by comparison.

My good friend, producer of the series Richard Mervyn, said to me of physics, 'Oh, that's all Boyle's Law, batteries and balances.' On the contrary, here were people who saw the universe around us in such a strange, imaginative and compelling way that ordinary laboratory apparatus and hardware almost vanished in the power of their imagination and experiment.

The second strand to my story therefore is unexpected. It is not that the study of the paranormal has moved closer to science, but the best and most innovative of science has clearly taken a very large step towards a view of the universe which finds nothing at all outrageous in the idea that minds can communicate with matter or that minds can affect matter or minds affect minds.

Figs. 1, 2, 3
Three of the men who were part of the revolution in physics, realising that it was not merely the study of a mechanical reality. From left to right: Niels Bohr, the Dane; Erwin Schrödinger, the German physicist; Paul Dirac, the French mathematician. For a picture of Einstein, see Fig. 20.

The making of the television series and the making of this book were both a hugely enjoyable voyage of discovery for me, as I hope they will be for you. To have written a complete account of the subject, I would have needed at least five volumes. I have concentrated instead on the most reliable and best documented experiments in the subject, and have put together a list of further reading, to be found at the end of the book, so that you can pursue in greater depth any particular part that interests you. Having opened with the ground rules of a good experiment, I conclude with an appendix suggesting ways in which you can carry out your own experiments into the paranormal and perhaps discover these abilities in yourself or others.

Finally, I think I should declare my own attitude to the paranormal. Having finished my investigation, my attitude is this:

A scientist would have to be either massively ignorant or a confirmed bigot to deny the evidence that the human mind can make connection with space, time and matter in ways which have nothing to do with the ordinary senses. Further, he cannot deny that these connections are compatible with current thinking in physics, and may in the future become accepted as a part of an extended science, in which the description 'paranormal' no longer applies, and can be replaced by 'normal'.

Here is an account of my own investigation.

1. Evidence, Experiments and Bigots

My first suggestion to you is this: do not accept what you see. Let me explain.

Arthur Ellison is Professor of Electrical Engineering at the City University of London. Not only is he an excellent scientist, but he possesses a resolute sense of humour. He has been interested in the paranormal for most of his life, and he recently gave a lecture on the subject to a mixed audience of scientists and non-scientists. Towards the end of his talk, he asked the audience to participate in an experiment.

Next to him on the rostrum was a bowl of flowers on a table. Much to the dismay of the audience, he asked them to concentrate collectively on the bowl of flowers to see whether they could levitate it. With some pitying smiles and anxious frowns, the audience eventually began to concentrate. The professor said that to help them he was going to play a tape-recording of the Buddhist chant 'ommm', a sound which is supposed to make the whole universe change.

The concentration of the audience grew deeper, the lecture hall was pervaded with the ominous droning sound of the chant. Slowly at first, gradually more rapidly, the bowl of flowers began to wobble, and finally it left the surface of the table and floated clear, several millimetres in the air. Levitation!

The audience drew back aghast at their achievement. Without warning, the bowl of flowers crashed down to the table; immediately the audience broke up in a furious buzz of conversation. What had happened?

The point of my story is *not* the levitation, but that two people came up to Professor Ellison afterwards. One was an old lady, the other a professor of physics.

The old lady said, 'Do you know, Professor, when the bowl of flowers lifted I saw a grey substance between the bowl and the table and between the legs of the table and the floor.'

The professor of physics snorted derisively. 'I don't know what all the fuss was about, *nothing* moved at all!'

Fig. 4
Professor Arthur
Ellison, Professor of
Electrical Engineering
at City University,
London, taking part in
the reconstruction of
the levitation
experiment, which was
carried out for the
filming. The
participants are
'meditating'; the bowl
has lifted clear of the
table.

Actually, the bowl of flowers *did* move and *did* levitate, because the professor had hidden special magnets in the bowl and under the table. He had played the Buddhist chant of 'ommm' to hide the humming noise of the electromagnets. However, and this is really what assessing the paranormal is about, the old lady *saw* a grey substance, but there was *no* grey substance; the professor saw *nothing* move, when something *did* move. The vision of both lady and professor was completely faulty.

Lord Reith was once accused of employing biased broadcasters in the BBC. His reply was: 'I am glad to be able to tell you that *none* of my broadcasters is free of bias.'

In the field of the paranormal there has been more irrational bias and more furious, vindictive and downright nasty criticism than in any other field of scientific investigation. Scientists, clerics, writers and mystics have all pitched in with a ferocity which would do credit to a street gang and which has nothing at all to do with science, reason or evidence. Why?

If, as I now accept, there *is* something there in the paranormal, it is potentially the most important and optimistic development in the whole field of human knowledge. Instead of having to accept the view that we are just fleshly beings in a materialistic and mechanical universe, the paranormal allows us, if it is valid, to accept, as reasonable beings, that there is much more to the human mind, the human condition and the universe around us.

This view threatens a lot of people who defend a particular view of things. It upsets the vested interest of some clerics who hold to a dogmatic theological standpoint; it upsets some scientists who wish to preserve a mechanistic picture of the universe; it upsets some writers who prefer an unshakeably sceptical position, because it means that they do not have to try to extend their view of things, and can remain in the relatively comfortable role of permanently Doubting Thomases. There are, fortunately, just as many clerics, scientists and writers who do preserve critical but properly open minds.

There are three main ways of acquiring knowledge: by direct experience, by reason, and by authority. I will deal with the first two later, but it is knowledge by authority that the paranormal threatens. Knowledge by authority is no more than, 'I say it is so, my own colleagues agree that it is so, and so it is so.' A good example of this way to knowledge was told to me by a professor of physics in Vienna.

When the idea of meteorites arriving on the earth from space was first suggested, it was clearly impossible, because the planets had been found to move in regular ellipses: nothing broke out of a regular ellipse. A statement was put out by the ruling scientists: 'Anyone who holds the irrational view that meteorites originate in space shall suffer expulsion from our learned society of astronomers.'

Later, when the evidence for the actual, extra-terrestrial origin of meteorites had become completely overwhelming, a statement was again put out: 'Anyone who holds to the irrational view that meteorites originate on earth shall suffer expulsion from our learned society of astronomers.' No one blushed. Most thinkers want to belong to a club of like thinkers; it feels cosy.

My suggestion is that you should adopt the view of Groucho Marx, who remarked: 'Any club who would have me as a member, I wouldn't want to belong to.' Think for yourself, do not join a club. What can you think, what can you believe? The *Oxford Dictionary* defines 'believe' as 'have faith in ...' or 'accept the truth of ...'. If someone says 'there is a God', that is a statement of belief. If another says 'there is no God', that is also a statement of belief, because both people have faith in what they said. Neither statement is susceptible to analysis, measurement or solution.

To take a simpler example, if someone says, 'I believe I can predict the future,' that is a belief which can be examined and checked. If a large number of people claimed (as they did) that they predicted the sinking of the *Titanic*, then these claims alone are no more than statements of belief: 'I believe I predicted the sinking of the *Titanic*.'

If, on the other hand, you were an author called Morgan Robertson who wrote a novel some twelve years before the *Titanic* actually went down, in which you imagined a fictional liner called the *Titan* sinking, your novel might have achieved decent obscurity unless you also described the following points about your fictional liner which were nearly the same for the *Titanic*:

	SS *Titan*	SS *Titanic*
Number of lifeboats	24	20
Speed at impact with iceberg	25 knots	23 knots
Tonnage	75,000 tons	66,000 tons
Length overall	800 feet	882·5 feet
Number of propellers	3	3
Collision with iceberg	Yes	Yes
Myth of unsinkability	Yes	Yes
Month of sinking	April	April

We are now in a much better position to interpret the statement 'I believe Morgan Robertson predicted the sinking of the *Titanic* some twelve years before it actually did sink.' The novel was a matter of documentary record in 1898, the year of publication. Did Morgan Robertson predict the future?

When scientists look for similarities between pairs of events and things, they talk about 'correlations' between them. This is really no more than saying that they are looking at the patterns of similarity between them. Looking at the similarities between the fictional SS *Titan* and the real life SS *Titanic*, there are a large number of correlations by any standards. We can begin to suspect that Morgan Robertson actually did predict the sinking of a liner twelve years before it happened. But did he?

We can now ask more useful questions. Were the details of the *Titanic* design known in 1895, when the novel was being written? They were not in fact, but there are other questions which help us to evaluate the extremely odd correlations. Were there general principles of ship design around at the time which might have enabled the author to make a fairly detailed guess as to its design? Yes, there were; but were these detailed enough to get that number of correlations? I don't think they were, but others disagree. The mythological name *Titan* has often been used for describing something large, so this could have also been coincidence. But was it? The number of lifeboats per ton weight might also have been a fixed relationship agreed among ship designers and so the author could have been almost right on this score, just by researching his book carefully.

What seems at first sight to be a clearly paranormal prediction now begins to come under question, but the questions do not invalidate the *possibility* that Morgan Robertson did in fact see a future event before it happened; they simply stop us rushing in and making too many assumptions. If you would like to study the Titanic story in more detail, there are more detailed accounts to be studied. [1, 2, 3]

What the questions achieve is that they force us to make ground rules for the evaluation of reports like this, so that anything we do finally accept as paranormal is likely to be as a result of a stringent application of reason and analysis.

G. W. Lambert, in the *Journal of the Society of Psychical Research* [4], suggested that when studying a prediction:

1 The prediction should be reported to a credible witness before the event to which it appears to relate.
2 The time interval between the prediction and the event should be short.
3 The connection between the person making the prediction and the prediction itself should be improbable.
4 The prediction should be described literally and not symbolicly.
5 The *details* of the prediction should tally with the *details* of the event.

Next time a friend tells you that they dreamt about an air crash and an air crash occurs shortly after the dream, ask these questions and see how accurately predictive the dream really was. Even when the questions have been asked though, there will always be an element of uncertainty. Just *how* good were the correlations between prediction and event? The 'how' is one of the great problems associated with claims in the paranormal.

If your friend predicts an air crash and one occurs shortly afterwards this is not especially interesting by itself, because a future air crash is a near certainty, and people often dream about

[1] A. Mackenzie, *Riddle of the Future*, Arthur Barker, London, 1974

[2] I. Stephenson, *Journal of the American Society for Psychical Research*, vol. 54, 1960

[3] L. C. Robertson, *Journal of the Society for Psychical Research*, vol. 39, 1957

[4] G. W. Lambert, *Journal of the Society for Psychical Research*, vol. 43, 1965

things that frighten them, like air travel. But if they get the time, the aircraft type, the flight number and the casualties all correct, or partly correct, within the rules I have suggested, then it is reasonable to assume a connection between the mind of the dreamer and a future event. There are many such accounts in the literature referred to above. [1, 2, 3]

The doubt always remains, however, with anecdotal evidence. Can investigators do better? Yes, because they can design and perform *experiments*. What is an experiment, and what constitutes a good or bad experiment?

An experiment is a *test* of an idea, where the *outcome* of the test is not known. A good experiment is a test where all possible ways of explaining the idea have been looked for and one is selected as true and to be tested, and where all the methods used are fully declared for other people to assess and to repeat.

A bad experiment is a test where these conditions have not been met and where doubts and loopholes remain unanswered or undeclared. For example, returning to the metal-bending example I used in the introduction, if an investigator is taken into a room where a subject is sitting holding a teaspoon which he is stroking and the teaspoon bends downwards and the bowl drops off the handle as he strokes it, this is a thoroughly *bad* experiment because the subject could have used a special teaspoon (as I did in the television programme) or he could have almost broken it secretly by hand and then completed the break when he stroked it.

A good experiment would be as follows: a teaspoon is bought in a shop by the investigator; it is carefully examined by a metallurgist and marked, then presented to the subject under the continuous view of the investigator and a number of disinterested observers and kept in *continuous* view by the investigator and observers as the subject attempts to bend it, ideally under filmed conditions. If at the end of the experiment, the spoon has bent, or broken, it is returned under *continuous* observation to the metallurgist. If both investigator and observers are satisfied from their observations and subsequent study of the film that the subject could not have bent the spoon with his fingers, then it would be reasonable to say either that the subject bent the spoon paranormally, or that there was collusion or fraud between investigator and subject, or between investigator, subject and observers.

If the subject can repeat the bending and the investigator writes up his experiment in sufficient detail for the other people to repeat it exactly, then paranormal metal bending could be said to be proved beyond reasonable doubt.

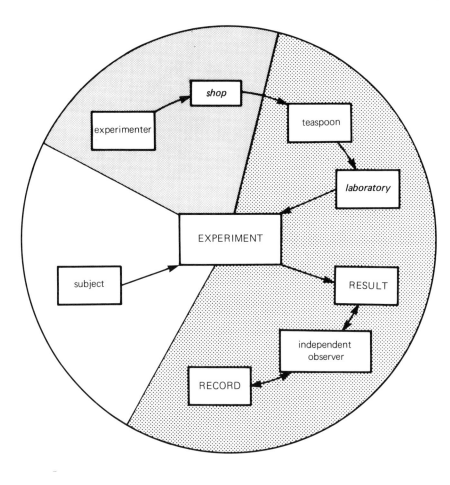

Fig. 5
To perform a good
experiment on metal
bending, the minimum
necessary
requirements are that
an experimenter buys a
spoon, marks it so it
can be identified
again, and takes it to a
laboratory where it is
kept in continuous
view by the
experimenter and an
independent observer.
The subject is admitted
to the laboratory only
at the time of the
experiment, and the
spoon is still kept
under continuous
observation. Results
are assessed by the
independent observer
before they are finally
published.
Experimenter, subject
and observer maintain
their independence, as
shown in the different
shading in the
diagram.

There are, as I shall show, an increasing number of very cautious investigators who are examining paranormal metal bending under conditions as tight or tighter than those I have already suggested.

But what about collusion and fraud? Does it occur? Yes, it does, I am afraid – but not only in the field of the paranormal. It also occurs in ordinary laboratories and among ordinary jobbing scientists. J. B. Rhine, one of the founders of experiments into the paranormal, found thirteen clear cases of cheating, [5] and others have since come to light. Yet in 1976 Ian St James Roberts conducted a survey of cheating among ordinary scientists. [6] To the great surprise of both academics and other professionals, a substantial proportion of scientists, it was found, knew of at least one colleague who had consciously or unconsciously fiddled his results.

I can remember filling in the questionnaire the study was based on. One question was effectively: have you ever spotted a scientist

[5] J. B. Rhine, *Journal of Parapsychology*, vol. 38, 1974

[6] I. St James Roberts, *New Scientist*, vol. 72, 1976 (two articles, pp. 466, 618)

cheating? I wrote: 'Yes'. The colleague whom I had seen cheating did so on such a massive and unlikely scale that first of all I simply could not believe it, but it was true nevertheless. He is now a senior professor. He was certainly deluding himself, but I am not exactly sure to this day whether he was deliberately deluding others as well. His basic problem was an absolutely compulsive personal ambition.

There is one striking difference between cheating in ordinary science and cheating among experimenters on the paranormal. In ordinary science, as St James Roberts points out, 80 per cent of those caught cheating received no public punishment and some continued to be promoted. But where experimenters on the paranormal are concerned, all thirteen were cut out of the field of research altogether and their work publicly registered as dubious unless it could be repeated. An excellent review of cheating in science and the paranormal is to be found in the work of an experimental psychologist Dr Charles Tart. [7]

[7] C. Tart, *Psi*, E. P. Dutton, New York, 1977

There clearly has been cheating in experiments on the paranormal. This has been used by a number of people as a total explanation of all paranormal phenomena. This is a perfectly legitimate point of view, but it is one which is rarely applied to ordinary scientific research and which has now been carried to a quite unreasonable extreme.

One critic began his examination of the paranormal with the statement: 'In view of the *a priori* arguments against it, we know in advance that telepathy etc. cannot occur.' [8] Another referee for an article on the paranormal submitted to a scientific journal said, 'This is the kind of thing that I would not believe in even if it existed.' [9]

[8] C. E. M. Hansel, *ESP: a Scientific Evaluation*, Scribner, New York, 1966

[9] Quoted in R. Targ and H. Puthoff, *Mind-Reach*, Delacorte, New York, 1977; Jonathan Cape, London, 1977

A conjurer called The Amazing Randi has issued a challenge, promising 10,000 dollars to anyone who can: '. . . demonstrate any paranormal ability under satisfactory observing conditions.' I wrote to him asking for his conditions and, having studied them, I am persuaded that no one can possibly adhere to the conditions he lays down under any experimental circumstances whatever.

There is also a Committee for the Scientific Investigation of Claims of the Paranormal which performs the valuable function of doubting all claims to paranormal effect. Such criticism, when detailed, particular, and properly analytical, is an essential part of the search for reliable data, but unfortunately this committee has also repeatedly spilled over into rhetoric, invective and non-specific generalities and has entirely spoiled its reputation among ordinary scientists by failing to get to grips with the mass of experimental data which is publicly available.

On the reverse side of the coin there is a very large number of completely gullible people in the field who accept absolutely everything they hear about the paranormal, from sharpening razor blades under pyramids to UFOs from Atlantis.

Both sides of this polemic and unreasonable divide have no place at all in any rational assessment of the paranormal, and can be safely ignored.

We now need to examine another feature of the world about us before arming ourselves with the means to judge claims in the paranormal. Two words are important – 'luck' and 'chance'. 'Luck' means nothing more than good fortune, and yet it is often used about people. A punter is said to be lucky if he wins regularly at the races, but the word itself has no explanatory meaning. It doesn't tell us *how* or *why* he wins.

'Chance', on the other hand, is more useful. If I toss a coin, then, after a large number of tries, I will find that it comes down 50 per cent heads and 50 per cent tails. Supposing I then ask someone to guess whether the coin will land heads or tails while the coin is still in the air; that someone is normally going to be right by *chance* 50 per cent of the time. Therefore if they make 100 guesses, they should be right 50 times by *chance*.

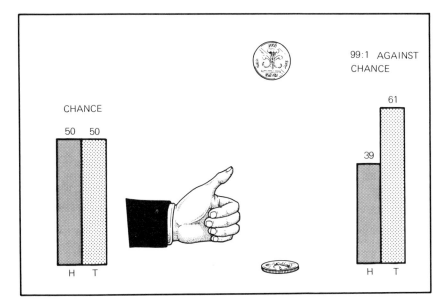

Fig. 6
When a coin is tossed, it should come down 50 per cent heads and 50 per cent tails if enough trials are made. The result of each toss is independent of any other. If the results consistently depart from 50:50, we should look for a cause. If a coin comes down 39 heads and 61 tails in 100 trials, the results of that happening by chance alone are 99 to 1 against.

If another person, say, gets 61 guesses right, that is well above chance and would only happen *once* in 100 guesses, so you can say that the odds against getting 61 right by chance are 99 to 1 against. There is a fixed mathematical relationship between the number of correct guesses in a run and the odds of that number occurring by chance. If someone regularly got this sort of score under the sort of experimental conditions I have outlined then it would be reasonable to search for a cause.

For example, it would be entirely reasonable to investigate the possibility that the subject was either 'seeing' into the immediate future of the coin or influencing the coin directly with his mind – that is, if he had not substituted an artificially loaded coin. This is why I am going to move next onto the story of the new physics. To see into the future or to influence metal with the mind is by the rules and standards of the old physics *absolutely* impossible. It simply cannot happen, and yet it is the firmly held view of many of the world's most able physicists that such connections *are* possible. So, I am going to look at some of the changes in physics which have created this complete revolution in ideas about how the universe works and how the mind can connect with matter.

2. Physics: Sense and Nonsense

Physics, to most people, is a completely commonsense, logical and rational subject. But I am sorry to have to tell you that as you get deeper into the book, to understand what the new physics is now saying, I am going to ask you to take leave of the common senses that you use in everyday life. Remember this: I shall also only use words in their correct and actual meaning, and so 'senses' and 'common senses' are exactly what I mean here. But why should I ask you to do anything so silly? What can be wrong with the senses? They obviously work very well. Sight, hearing, touch and taste all guide us around the practical, everyday world with the greatest accuracy.

Our eyes tell us in what direction to walk, we can identify a noise with our ears; we touch an object to find out what it feels like; we can easily tell sugar from vinegar with our tongues. Self-confidence in everyday life depends absolutely on the senses, so there is no use asking you to give them up unless there is an absolutely overwhelming need to do so.

There is.

The new physics has revealed such a magnificently absurd structure to the world about us, that our commonsense mind and its senses cannot possibly appreciate it as a simple, visual, tactile, mechanical picture. This is not some wild fancy of the scientists; experiments show conclusively that it is there. The other problem about the new physics is that you often hear the cry of despair, 'Oh, that's all too difficult for me,' or, 'Only ten people in the whole world understand that.'

Both comments are nonsense, and have probably been suggested by physicists who don't want to understand it either. So my next assertion is that the basic ideas of physics can be happily and completely understood by people who can read and who can understand the words to be found in the *Oxford Dictionary*.

I do not mean that I can turn you into an instant mathematician, but what you *can* do, if you like, is to understand as completely as *any* physicist alive today what the essential ideas of physics mean to us as ordinary curious and wondering human beings, and how those ideas are starting to validate what we now call 'paranormal'.

If I now claim that 'matter has only a tendency to exist', you will either consign this book to the waste-basket or hire a psychiatrist and have me put away. If I also claim that 'no scientist can study the properties of anything', you could have me put in a straitjacket as well. But since I *am* going to make these statements a little later on in the book, I had better lay in some groundwork quickly.

Why do we need to understand the ideas of this new physics? Because they are providing a consistent, logical and problem-solving view of the universe which is beginning to show signs of compatibility with the strange events we now call paranormal. As I have already stated that by the rules of the old physics, the paranormal is by definition impossible. It cannot exist.

So what was the old physics? It has often been called 'Newtonian physics' because it is based upon the ideas of one of the most innovative men of science who have ever lived, Sir Isaac Newton, a genius who also had the modesty to exclaim, 'I succeeded only because I have been able to stand on the shoulders of giants.'

The old, or Newtonian, physics believed the universe to be one of predictable, commonsense certainty. Heavenly bodies moved with a magnificent and ponderous evenness; the behaviour of large objects and things seemed to be perfectly understood. It was a universe of the engineer where all phenomena could be visualised by the senses and where it was believed that all knowledge could be complete.

It has sometimes been referred to as the 'universe of God the clockmaker'. And so, in the clockmakers' view of things, biological clockwork mechanisms like brains simply could not communicate; there was simply no place at all in that physics for such a strange event to occur. A physicist might have said: 'There is no place in our general model for such phenomena.'

All science consists of making models, to see then what fits into the model and what fails to do so. Most phenomena – a *phenomenon* is only something of which the senses are aware – fitted into the Newtonian view of things, and minds communicating either with other minds or with matter itself simply did not.

Remember the furious disclaimer from a scientist about the paranormal which I quoted in the previous chapter: 'I wouldn't believe it, even if it were true.' This extraordinary example of prejudice can now be more easily understood; the paranormal simply did not fit into this particular scientist's model of the universe, and so he rejected it like the professor of physics and the bowl of flowers.

In 1895 a German scientist was experimenting with an electrical machine inside a wooden box. Each time he switched it on, a screen some feet away from the box glowed brightly. When he turned the machine off, the glow on the screen died away. In those days, it was basic dogma that nothing went through wood without making a hole. There were *no* holes in the wood, and so nothing passed through it. But *something* did.

Three weeks later, the scientist called Wilhelm Röntgen had named the something 'X-rays', and taken the first photograph of the bones of his hand. In 1901 he received the Nobel Prize. His senses told him one thing, but his analytical intelligence told him another. What he discovered was *nonsense* in terms of the then accepted picture of the world.

A French scientist called Henri Becquerel placed uranium crystals on top of a sealed photographic plate; the plate was fogged. Again it was dogma that nothing could pass through the seals. But *something* did. He had discovered natural radioactivity, and presaged the atomic age. His discovery, too, was 'nonsensical'.

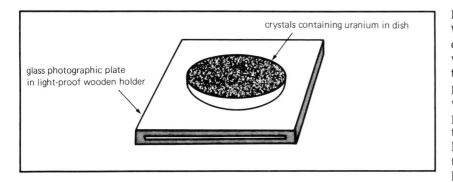

crystals containing uranium in dish

glass photographic plate in light-proof wooden holder

One of the biggest surprises I can remember was when I began to read what the best of the new physicists were saying about the world and the universe.

Physics is a tough, hard-edged sort of subject, and it deals with tough, hard-edged things like metals, pieces of wood, atoms and planets. Yet when I looked at what physicists were writing about matter, time and the human mind, it seemed to me that they were sounding more like mystics than scientists. To my commonsense mind, what they were saying sounded almost irrational. Then I thought, 'Well, every subject has its cranks, and this is probably a small group of scientists who have formed a mutual admiration society, and are telling each other pleasant fantasies. Scientist science-fiction writers perhaps.'

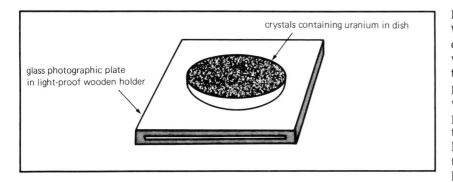

Fig. 7
When crystals containing uranium were left in a dish on top of a photographic plate sealed in a wooden plate case, the plate was exposed as though it had been in light. It was received truth at the time this happened in Henri Becquerel's laboratory, that nothing could go through wood without making a hole. But something *had* gone through, and Becquerel persisted with this reasoning, to discover radioactivity.

What is so important about the paranormal? Why should we bother to study its connection with the new physics. The answer is what we found while we were making the television series: that there are unknowns in the universe which can only be solved by assuming a connection between mind and matter, mysteries which suggest that we are very much more than the sum of our parts. So, what I have to tell you is optimistic for that reason alone.

I also realised that a high proportion of the scientists making these strange comments were either Nobel Prize winners or they had achieved the full approval of their peers as physicists and not as cranks. I began to study the implications of what they were saying. I found that they had taken an extraordinary and exciting leap in the dark and found such fascinating and totally strange aspects of the world about us that their view of things sounded more like poetry. In short, that the best of the new physics was akin to the best of creative art and was little to do with 'Boyle's Law, batteries and balances'. This was certainly a very exciting discovery for me: that the best available minds in the hardest of hard sciences were suggesting that there could be real links between paranormal events and the material substance of the universe.

These links are what this book is about. It is not only the mystics who think there is a connection between mind and matter; the physicists are beginning to say very much the same thing. Professor Brian Josephson, Nobel Laureate in physics in 1973, has written: ' "Psychic Phenomena" violate some of our conceptions about space, time and causation. But so does "current physics". [I have put 'current physics' in place of 'quantum mechanics' which is what Professor Josephson actually wrote, since this refers to a specific part of the new physics.] It is not too far-fetched to say that if psychic phenomena had not been found experimentally, they might have been predicted by an imaginative theoretician.' [1]

It is not that the Newtonian 'clockwork' view of the universe was wrong; it was simply that it revealed serious gaps and discrepancies which had to be filled. New discoveries do not necessarily invalidate the old ones. Professor Josephson again: 'If psychic phenomena are a reality, would it mean the overthrow of conventional physics? Hardly. The history of science shows clearly that new phenomena do not have to invalidate the old physics.' [1]

I have made the outlandish claim that the new physics sounds more like the mystics talking. What evidence have I?

Dr Lawrence Le Shan is a highly articulate and ebulliently human scientist who made several important contributions to our

[1] B. Josephson, *The Iceland Papers*, Essentia Research Associates, Wisconsin, 1979

Fig. 8
Dr Lawrence Le Shan,
former head of the
Department of
Psychology at the
Trafalgar Hospital and
Institute of Applied
Biology, New York. He
investigated the
similarity between the
views of the world
held by two
distinguished groups,
one of physicists, one
of mystics.

programmes. He is also an experimental psychologist of great experience and he carried out the following test.

He made short extracts from the writings of about sixty people as to how they saw the nature of the universe. Thirty were from contemporary scientists and thirty were from mystics. He then extracted certain key words from the descriptions such as 'electron' or 'Brahma', which would have given the game away, and then showed the descriptions to a group of people and asked them who wrote which. No one could say. No one could distinguish a description of the universe by a mystic from a description by a scientist. Here are some examples: can you distinguish who wrote what?

1 'It is the mind which gives things their quality their foundation and their being.'
2 'The stuff of the world is mind-stuff.'
3 'The universe looks less and less like a great machine and more and more like a great thought.'
4 'Pure logical thinking cannot yield us any knowledge of the empirical world; all knowledge of reality starts from experience and ends in it. Propositions arrived at by purely logical means are completely empty of reality.'

5 'It is necessary therefore, that advancing knowledge should be based on a clear, pure and disciplined intellect.'* [2]

As I will suggest at the end of the book, Dr Le Shan's views form an important cornerstone in what could turn out to be a general theory of the paranormal, but for the present his experiment

[2] L. Le Shan, *The Medium, the Mystic and the Physicist*, Turnstone Books, London, 1974

Fig. 9
Sir James Jeans (1877–1946), a mathematician who applied mathematics to astronomy. It was he who described the universe as 'less and less like a great machine and more and more like a great thought'.

revolutionised my view of how the best of current physicists are thinking. They are not confining their attention to the energies and hardware of the universe, but instead they are thinking in ways which are just as innovative as any other creative and imaginative human being.

There is however, one vital difference between a mystic and a physicist. No one can *prove* that a mystic had a thoroughly bad idea or that a painter painted a very bad picture; but one scientist can often be proved totally wrong by another who points out one insurmountable flaw in his logic or experiment. So if the new physics has arrived at such a complex and fascinating view of the universe it was not only by creative insight, it was also by hard, rigorous and unbending experiment and proof. As I shall show you later in the book, current physics has arrived at the following completely astonishing conclusions:

* 1 Dhammapada, mystic
2 Sir Arthur Eddington, physicist
3 Sir James Jeans, physicist
4 Albert Einstein, physicist
5 Sri Aurobinde, mystic

1 Space and time are elastic, changeable qualities.
2 Space and time are different according to *where* you are.
3 Physics cannot study reality but only the connection between

the mind of the experimenter and the system he experiments on.

4 The act of measurement may change the object being measured.
5 The assumption of cause always preceding effect may not apply in all cases.
6 Objects and events which are to our senses separate in space, may in fact be connected in a real and functional way.
7 An 'absolute reality' is probably non-existent.

These new views completely change our everyday view of the world around us, and provide a growing intellectual structure which can help us to understand some of the puzzling phenomena of the paranormal. Physics ideas do apply to everyday events. Physics is not an esoteric subject confined to *laboratory* phenomena, but one which attempts to describe the macroscopic (large-scale) world of which our senses perceive a part. It would be premature to suppose that they completely explain it, but they do indicate a world view in which the paranormal is both likely and possible.

Armed with this introduction to the new physics, I want now to look at some experiments which claim to show that some people can, without using their ordinary senses, 'see' what is happening tens of miles away from where they are.

3. Things Remotely Seen

When I look at the sun, I claim that my eyes are receiving a picture of an object 93 million miles away. Neither the old nor the new physics has any quarrel with that.

If two physicists do experiments to show that someone can 'see' some miles over the horizon and discover what other people are looking at, the supporters of the old physicists state categorically: 'This cannot happen; our model does not allow it.' The new physicists, on the other hand, say: 'Yes, it is conceivable, but you had better produce some good hard evidence to prove it.'

Dr Russell Targ and Dr Harold Puthoff are two highly qualified physicists who work at Stanford Research Institute in California and they have, for the past seven years or so, been doing carefully designed experiments on what has become known as 'remote viewing'. I say to you: Lock someone up in a room; take ten other people, drive them ten miles to a secret destination and let them wander around; then ask the person in the locked room to describe and draw what the others are looking at ten miles away.

If the someone did so successfully, you would quite rightly make very suspicious noises and suggest that some of these possibilities might have occurred:

1 The two groups got together before the experiment and arranged matters so that their descriptions tallied.
2 The person in the locked room had been given the location of the 'secret' destination beforehand.
3 The fit between what the person in the locked room described and what the other group were actually looking at was bad.
4 There was at least one 'mole' in one of the two places who was spying for the others, a sort of telepathic double-O-seven, a very *normal* fiddler.
5 The scientists running the experiments were all liars and frauds.
6 It might have happened once and would not stand up to attempts at repetition.

I opened by stating that this book is about the connections between mind and matter, and is not a report on the assertions of cranks. We are going to need this sort of criticism to help decide about a particular claim that something is 'paranormal' in the sense that I use the word.

So I now want to look at what Drs Targ and Puthoff actually did to get around these criticisms in their own experiments in California. Both are highly experienced laboratory scientists and have spent much of their lives in discovering the tricks and pitfalls of experimental work in a laboratory. Puthoff has worked in research optics and quantum electronics and Targ has specialised in high-power laser research, microwave physics, and the development of the plasma laser. They finally came up with a scheme that answers the objections I have just mentioned. Experimental schemes are called 'protocols' by scientists. The word originally meant 'the original draft of diplomatic document', but it is used here to mean 'the detailed account of experimental method'.

First of all they make up a 'pool' of more than one hundred different map references of locations. Then, after 'shuffling' or randomising these one hundred locations, one is selected 'blind' by one member of the research team.

Another member of the team has meanwhile gone to the laboratory and has locked himself up with the person who is going to do the 'remote viewing', as they call it. He has no communication with the experimenter who has selected the target location blind, who now gives an envelope with the sealed location to another experimenter, who drives the group of people who are going to

Fig. 10
Remote viewing involves two people and independent judges. Having synchronised their watches, one person is given a target location to visit; the other remains at the lab. Both – the viewer is called 'outbound' and the one at the lab 'inbound' – are kept under surveillance. At an appointed time, the person at the target location is asked to 'transmit' mental images of the location to the subject in the lab, who draws and tape-records his mental impressions. After the experiment is complete, photographs of the target and the impressions of the subject in the lab are given to independent judges, who alone decide if there is any match.

laboratory

remote viewing

remote viewing site

inbound team

outbound team

independent judge

use their real eyes to view the target. On the way, driving out of the laboratory, they open the sealed envelope and drive to the location it contains.

What do we have? One experimenter selects the location from a randomised series. He gives it sealed to a second experimenter who takes the 'real viewing' group to the location.

A third experimenter, at a pre-arranged time, tells the 'remote viewing' person ('inbound' person) back in the laboratory to record what the 'real viewing' group ('outbound' group) are looking at. This the inbound person does on audio tape and by making sketches. None of the experimenters is told anything of what the others know. Finally, the 'real viewing' group return to the laboratory with photographs of the target.

The photographs, the tape recordings and the drawings are again put into separate envelopes, shuffled and randomised, and given to yet another experimenter who judges 'hits' between photographs and blind descriptions, and gives them a score. He also finally visits the location to verify the accuracy of the photographs.

Let us now review the potential criticism:

1 *The 'real viewers' and the 'remote viewer' got together beforehand.* No, they were carefully kept apart and could not have done so.
2 *The 'remote viewer' had been given the location beforehand.* No, he had not, because he was already isolated while the target was selected.
3 *The fit between the description and the photographs was bad.* No, it was not, because the independent judge could successfully connect one with the other.
4 *There was a 'mole' in one of the two places.* No, because he would have been ineffective since he could not have informed once they were already separated and the sealed target location opened.
5 *The experimenters were all cheats and liars.* No, this would imply collusion between up to six experimenters, two groups of people and the Dean of the College, who on some occasions chose the randomised location himself.
6 *It happened once only.* No, it did not. Targ and Puthoff have done some hundreds of experiments and now four other groups elsewhere have repeated them independently and achieved broadly similar results.

What are the results? What do they regard as being a 'hit'?

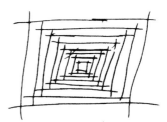

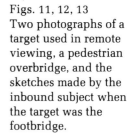

Figs. 11, 12, 13
Two photographs of a target used in remote viewing, a pedestrian overbridge, and the sketches made by the inbound subject when the target was the footbridge.

Fig. 14
Another remote viewing target, the Louisiana Superdome.

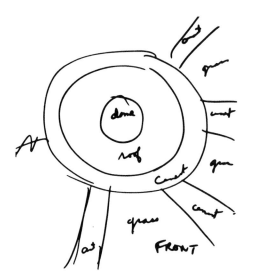
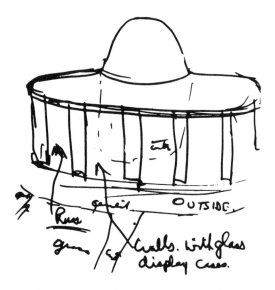

Fig. 15
The sketches made
when the target was
the Superdome.

As they showed in their published work, independent judges compared what the outbound (remote viewing) team saw and what the laboratory bound team either recorded on tape or sketched. They were able to match the two sets of data in a significant number of cases. The word 'significant' is used here in its statistical sense to mean: a numerical level which professional statisticians would agree indicates a result is not explicable by chance (see page 56).

Some experiments they carried out do not need detailed analysis. Providing one is satisfied that all the objections to these experiments which I have already mentioned were met, the identifications of the Louisiana Superdome and the iron framework of the footbridge are remarkable by any standards.

Other identifications proved to be far more difficult as I discovered by taking part in an experiment on remote viewing myself (see below).

Targ and Puthoff also discovered that each remote viewer adopted their own particular style of identification; each one had a 'signature' by which their attempts could be identified. Some people would sketch copiously and others would spend more time using the tape recorder. Others sometimes described things the wrong way round as seen in a mirror and a few described features which even the outbound team failed to see. For example, one subject described a belt drive at the top of a bench power drill which was not and could not have been seen by the outbound team who were actually operating the machine.

Most of the correct identifications relate to shape, form, colour and texture and do not involve specific names like 'Louisiana superdome' or 'iron footbridge'; they are usually in the form of what can only be called 'easily identifiable generalities' of the sort I have shown.

Remote viewing experiments are now being repeated at several other research centres in the United States, and similar results are being obtained. Once Targ and Puthoff had amassed sufficient data, they submitted their findings to two learned journals which publish research results from the more conventional sciences. [1, 2]

[1] R. Targ and H. Puthoff, *Proceedings of the Institute of Electronic and Electrical Engineers*, vol. 64, 1974

Very properly, their results were heavily criticised in very great detail. This is an entirely normal part of the scientific endeavour and often personally traumatic (as I know from my own experience) when one has one's own favourite ideas trampled to death in public. Research is an occupation which reminds me of President Truman's famous comment: 'If you can't stand the heat, stay out of the kitchen.'

[2] R. Targ and H. Puthoff, *Nature*, vol. 251, 1974

The point of these quite normal criticisms is that once they have been met, the work is accepted by rational scientists. Targ and Puthoff answered the criticisms in full, in my view, and have since gone on to write one book and contribute to another about remote viewing. [3, 4]

In the second of two books, they have themselves extended the criticisms of their own work by attacking their work themselves. On each count of criticism they have provided their own rebuttal.

[3] R. Targ and H. Puthoff, *Mind-Reach*, Delacorte, New York, 1977; Jonathan Cape, London, 1977

Apart from the criticisms in *Nature* and other similar approaches to their work, which are in the best tradition of science, there were also a crop of vindictive, irrational and often extremely silly attempts not to criticise their work, but to diminish their status and integrity as people. An excellent account of the 'debate' has been published. [3]

[4] R. Targ and H. Puthoff in C. Tart, H. Puthoff and R. Targ (eds.), *Mind at Large*, Praeger Scientific, New York, 1979

I now propose to add my own view of Russell Targ and Hal Puthoff. Having met them on several occasions and talked about science in general and remote viewing in particular with them, any suggestion that they are dupes, liars or frauds is totally risible. They are both people with an obvious and deeply seated integrity and devotion to the principles of research. In view, however, of some of the more opprobrious comment which has been made about them and their work, I would like here and now to pay tribute to their courage and persistence.

The experimental design they used may appear complex and difficult to understand, but it is based on a simpler procedure used in hospitals to test a new drug and it will be worthwhile giving a short account of this, so that the more technical aspects of their work can more easily be understood.

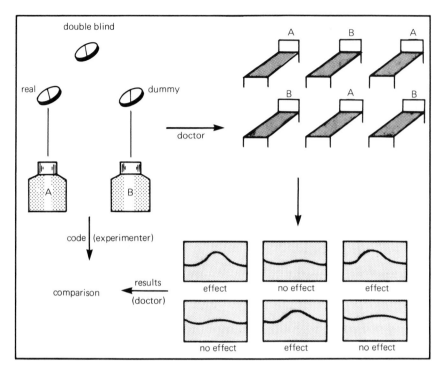

Fig. 16
The experimental design of a double blind experiment. The real pill and an identical dummy are given secret codes by the pharmacist (experimenter). The coded pills, some dummy, some real, are given to the patients by the doctor. The doctor records any changes in the patients' conditions, but he does not know which patients have been receiving real pills, and which dummy. When clinical trials are complete, only then do the doctor and pharmacist compare notes. A similar technique is used by some experimenters in the paranormal, to avoid accusation of fraud or collusion.

If I take the pills of a new drug into the ward and give them to patients, I can be accused of the faults I have already mentioned. For example, if I talk to the patients before I give them the pills, they could get better by suggestion; this is well known to occur. If I want to be famous for the discovery of the drug, I could fiddle my observations to show the best result.

The rules therefore get more rigorous. I must give the new drug to the hospital pharmacist who makes up some identical pills of chalk. He then gives me back two bottles, one containing the drug and the other the chalk. He knows from the code on the bottles which is which, but I do not. When I give the pills to the patients, I do not have any idea whether I am giving them chalk or drug.

I cannot fiddle my observations, because I do not know which patients had what – and so I do not know which patient is supposed to get better and which one isn't. I was *blind* to the effect, in other words.

Finally, the hospital pharmacist I gave the pills to tells me which pills were which and only then can we honestly compare notes about the effect of the pills. He was also *blind* to the effects of the pills he gave back to me. Therefore, the whole experiment is called a *double-blind trial*.

The experiments of Targ and Puthoff and many others are based upon double-blind techniques and in some of their work, 'multi-blind' experimental protocol was used where practically nobody knew what anyone else was doing except for one or two experimenters who had to correlate the results. For that reason alone, apart from the others which I have mentioned, collusion is an incredibly unlikely possibility.

However, collusion still continues to be levelled at work like this as a potential flaw, even though none has ever been shown. For example, [5] one critic wrote: 'If the result could have arisen through a trick, the experiment must be considered unsatisfactory proof of e.s.p., whether or not it is finally decided that such a trick was in fact used.'

[5] C. E. M. Hansel, *ESP: a Scientific Evaluation*, Scribner, New York, 1966

I am quite certain that the author of this statement has never applied this extraordinary standard of judgement to his own published research work, and in my own experience as a research scientist, I have never had to apply it to my own published papers.

It is, in my view, a stand of some desperation on the part of that particular critic if that is all he can think of as a potential flaw. Up to the time of writing, five other groups have continued work on 'remote viewing' and their results, so far, are broadly similar to those of Targ and Puthoff.

While we were making the television series, seeking to find out more for ourselves we decided to get everyone on the film team to participate in an *actual* remote viewing experiment. To do this we went to the Lawrence Berkeley Laboratories in California to meet and to work with Professor Elizabeth Rauscher.

Liz Rauscher is a Professor of Nuclear Science and Astrophysics working in the Lawrence Berkeley Laboratories. If that conjures an image of a blue stocking academic, you could not be more mistaken. She is, arguably, the most articulate and enthusiastic communicator about science that I have ever met, and apart from getting a bear-hug which regularly cracks a rib whenever I meet her, she is utterly tireless in her pursuit of very high level scientific conversation. She also laughs a great deal.

I recall one evening when Richard Mervyn, the Producer, and I were chatting away to her in a café in California. Neither Richard nor I are known for our conversational reticence but after some hours, and I do mean *hours*, of sparkling trialogue, we both began to flag from a combination of good wine and jet lag; Liz sailed on untiringly, revived every so often by injections of Coca-Cola. When finally we staggered out into the Californian night, I can remember that she looked slightly surprised that the evening had finished so early.

One of Targ and Puthoff's most successful remote viewing subjects is Hella Hammid. We had arranged with Liz Rauscher for me to take part in a remote viewing experiment with Hella. The film crew would be split into two groups; one with the outbound group and the other with the group remaining at the hotel.

The whole experiment was shot in real time with the watches of the two groups synchronised, and the film crew therefore acted as additional watchdogs. If there were any collusion or fraud, it would have to include Liz Rauscher, myself, Hella Hammid, the two film crews, the producer and Dr Beverley Rubik, a biologist who had joined us specifically for the experiment.

Hella Hammid is a professional photographer who began to work very reluctantly with Targ and Puthoff on remote viewing since she had no belief at all that it could work. It was initially much to her surprise that she became very successful at it. Now she is very confident about the ability and spends much of her time doing it.

It says much for the patience and sensitivity of Targ and Puthoff that they can get almost anyone to achieve remote viewing. At one time, they had a notice over their laboratory door which read: 'As you enter here you have permission to be psychic.' They recall that they once had a visit from an irate Pentagon official who stormed into their laboratory and said effectively, 'What the hell do you people think you're doing wasting government money on all this psychic rubbish.' A few days later he had participated in a successful remote viewing experiment. He left slightly chastened.

As we shall find out later in the book, successful paranormal activity is very much to do with how the subjects feel at the time and what sort of personality they have.

Here now is an account of our own remote viewing experiment, which we included in the television series.

Dr Beverley Rubik had selected six locations, and on the previous day had arranged with the owners of the properties that we should be allowed to visit each one with a television crew. Actually only one was to be visited. The names of all six locations were put into six sealed envelopes and the envelopes then locked unmarked into a steel box.

On the morning of the experiment, one television crew was locked into a hotel room with Hella Hammid and Liz Rauscher. The second television crew started filming Beverley and I as we walked to her car, our own watches been previously synchronised with the watches in the hotel room.

Beverley then handed me the locked steel box and operated a small random number generator to select a digit between one and six. I opened the locked box, counted down the pile of envelopes and selected the chosen one. I opened the envelope, showed the target location to Beverley, and we drove for about fifteen minutes to the site, the cameraman filming continuously in the back of the car.

The location selected was 'Indian Rock', a massive, rugged lump of rock with steps hewn into it which sticks out like a sore

Fig. 17
The target selected for the remote viewing experiment in which Kit Pedler took part: Indian Rock, Berkeley, an outcrop of rock in the middle of a residential district. Several points of correspondence with the inbound subject's report were noted, but there was an even closer correspondence to Codornices Park (Fig. 19). Kit is with Dr Beverley Rubik, a biologist who joined the team as a further guarantee against collusion.

thumb in the middle of a suburb in Berkeley. For the next thirty minutes, Beverley and I simply wandered up and down the rock relating to whatever feelings it generated in us at the time. We talked about these feelings and were filmed throughout.

At the end of the thirty-minute period, we drove back to the hotel, knocked at the door of the locked room, and were admitted by one of the film crew who had been designated the role of guarding the door to make sure that no one had entered or left since we had gone on our way to the target.

In summary, Dr Rubik and I acted as the outbound group, opening the location instruction having left the inbound group after synchronising watches. Two film crews acted as both recordists and watchdogs. Inbound and outbound experimenters met only after termination of a synchronised thirty-minute period.

We then all sat down with Liz Rauscher in the chair, and Beverley Rubik, Hella Hammid and I compared notes as to what

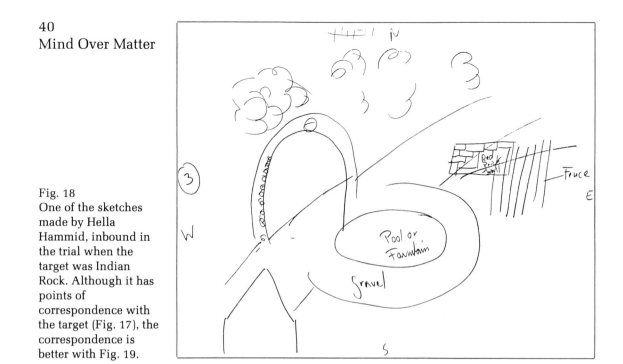

Fig. 18
One of the sketches
made by Hella
Hammid, inbound in
the trial when the
target was Indian
Rock. Although it has
points of
correspondence with
the target (Fig. 17), the
correspondence is
better with Fig. 19.

Fig. 19
Codornices Park. The
paths are gravel
covered, and descend
to a central pool.

Beverley and I had seen and experienced and what Hella had 'remotely' seen and experienced while we were outbound at the target.

As we looked at sketches and compared tape recordings, we gradually began to convince ourselves that the correspondence was fair to good. Then Hella went off with Beverley by car to visit all the locations to see whether she had 'been' where we had actually been. There was a tremendous atmosphere of expectancy as she came back into the room some forty-five minutes later.

She spoiled it all. Hella Hammid said quite decisively: 'I was not where you were, I was at Codornices Park.' After the feeling of disappointment, we talked it through again. Having looked at her notes and listened to her voice on tape I am persuaded that she was 'remotely' at Codornices Park and not at Indian Rock where we were.

It would have been splendid if we had achieved a 'hit'; it would have complemented the television series. The fact of the matter is that we did not.

But there are two genuinely strange aspects of this experiment. What happened when Hella Hammid identified another target on the list, but not the one we visited, is called by experimenters 'the displacement effect'. It is well known to occur, and Russell Targ tells me he is now experimenting actively on it as a separate part of the remote viewing problem. As I shall describe in a later section, I took part in another experiment in Cambridge where I achieved a quite remarkable 'displacement' identification. 'Displacement' is simply getting the wrong target right, when a selection of one target has been made from a 'pool' of targets.

Obviously, this is very suspicious. If an experimenter were to continue to compare a remote viewer's comments and sketches with enough target descriptions, sooner or later he would finally achieve a correspondence by chance alone, rather like the idea that a monkey with a typewriter would type the whole of Shakespeare by accident, if given a millennium to do it. It is of interest that the monkey and typewriter experiment has now been done by computer. The rather astonishing result was that in a length of time equal to the lifetime of the universe, the monkeys might achieve three or four consecutive words!

Hella's notes and sketches, however, do not need statistical analysis: the correspondence is enormous. A scientist, who taught me much of what I know, once said, 'Statistics should be used only for illumination and not proof.' In my opinion, she did remotely view Codornices Park.

The second really strange event that happened on the day of the experiment is this: the experiment was done at 3.30 in the afternoon. At 11.45 in the morning there had been concentrated activity in the hotel room while everyone prepared for the split-crew filming, which was difficult. During that, without knowing why, I asked everyone to be quiet and said very carefully that I was going to write something on a piece of paper and give it to Sally Barnsley, the production assistant on the series, for safe-keeping. This was done in front of eight people, the whole production team.

I have the note in front of me now. It reads: 'During the experiment, a part of the equipment will *inexplicably* fail.' The word inexplicably is underlined.

The random-number machine which Beverley operated as we got to the car at the beginning of the experiment at 3.10 in the afternoon failed. As she repeatedly tried to get it to produce a random number between one and six, it repeatedly showed the 'overload' sign in the number register. I asked Beverley whether she could explain this. She said, 'No, it has never done that before.' When she selected a number therefore, she did so by blindly pressing a number button on the calculator.

So the experiment was weak and untidy in many respects, but interesting in others. (I suppose it was too much to ask for to have a successful experiment, on the first trial on television.) Nevertheless, it remains absolutely clear to me that others can and do achieve successful 'remote viewing' identification.

Hella Hammid, for example, took part in an astonishing remote viewing experiment. She and another successful remote viewer, Ingo Swann, were asked to look at a marine map and try and 'see' remotely whether any wrecks were present on the sea bottom. The first interesting finding was that she and Swann both independently marked the same area on the map as containing a wreck.

The sea bottom of the area selected, near Catalina Island off north California, was then searched by submarine at a depth of 170 metres. A wreck was discovered. The possibility that the wreck had been previously registered was checked; it had not. All the other protocol faults that I mentioned earlier were all checked out. Further, Hella Hammid said before the search commenced, 'Somewhere you will find an obelisk; a large block.' A large block of masonry was discovered at the site. [4] The whole submarine operation was filmed and has been shown on American television. [6]

[6] CBS Television: 'Psychic Sea Hunt' in 'In Search of . . .' series. Researched by Steven Schwartz, produced by Jeffrey Pill.

Experiments on remote viewing are as well planned and executed as any in ordinary science, so what do they say? That some people under conditions of good rigorous control can 'see' or perceive something miles away with their mind's eye? If that really is a true result, I'm much more interested to know what happened and I want to get closer to the problem.

So, all I want to assume now is that information travels from one group of people distant from another, which, as we have seen, is *impossible* to the old physics and *nonsense* to the senses.

'Nonsense' means 'not perceivable by the senses' and this is the part of physics I want to look at next – the part which is not perceivable – because it will help towards understanding the strange results of remote viewing.

Supposing I use a radio transmitter and send a message to your receiver, we can agree that information travels from my set to yours and makes a noise in the loudspeaker of your set. That makes sense to our joint senses because we can experience the transmission in our mind's eye. Anyway, we've been told it happens, and it goes on happening *reliably*. However, if the new physics claims that information travel depends *where* you are and *when* you are, this is obviously non-sense because it conflicts with everyday sense experience.

If I sit and talk to a friend in my living room, I sit in one place and talk to him in another, and it does not at all depend on where he is or where I am in the room. Our conversation remains the same. We go on looking the same, the distance between us remains the same, our watches tell the same time, and the information I get from his voice is the same. We appear to know *absolutely* where we are and *absolutely* what time it is.

In Isaac Newton's day, the day of Newtonian physics, everyone would have agreed with this. Nature seemed hard-edged and commonsensical, and people believed that they could look at the world from an absolute position in space and describe absolute truths. It would take pressing reasons indeed for anyone to abandon this eminently practical and reliable view of things. Science changes only because it has to. Around the turn of this century, real problems *were* appearing in the old physics, which *demanded* change.

Russell Targ and Hal Puthoff carried out some careful experiments and are getting reliable results which are impossible by any commonsense standard. They show that some people can apparently detect what other people are seeing twenty miles away.

So, we appear to be talking about information travelling across space. We still need to know what happened. Was it brain radio, or do we have to call it 'psychic'?

I am not going to use the word 'psychic' any more in this book, because it does not help to explain impossible or non-sensical events. It says instead there is some sort of mysterious something

Fig. 20
One man who had the
courage not to accept
the prevailing view of
the world without
question: Albert
Einstein.

which we need to believe in and cannot therefore examine with an open mind.

We do not have to believe in anything yet, and we do not have to be fanatics for or against the paranormal. We simply have to retain and use some of the ground rules I sketched earlier on, and to retain an open mind about how the universe around us works.

You could immediately argue that I *believe* that Targ and Puthoff proved that people's minds can communicate. I don't *believe* it, but the evidence of their experiments shows that this *is* the most likely deduction. Now you could accuse me of playing with words, but my deduction is based on evidence and not on a vague magical power. I cannot reasonably fault their results, so I must accept them. What we have to do, above all, is to preserve an open mind. We can preserve an open mind by looking very closely at good experiments like these and not trusting to our senses. Good experiments describe everything the experimenter did and so other people can go out and repeat them.

Now we've established that, I want to demonstrate one of the great turning points of physics which changed fundamental ideas about the universe and brought physics to the point where it is now describing the universe in ways which will help us to understand how the paranormal might work.

Will it show how information gets around the place without the brain radios or psychic events? Yes, it might. To see that, however, we must begin at the beginning.

This man produced a theory in 1905 which set the whole world of commonsense, mechanical Newtonian physics on its head. It is called the Special Theory of Relativity.

Do not close the book!

The mere mention of the word 'relativity' has most people reaching for the panic button crying, 'It's too difficult for me,' or, 'Only ten people in the whole world understand it.' In fact, relativity is a stunningly beautiful and very *simple* idea, and you do not need maths or complicated apparatus to see what it means to our everyday way of looking at things. All the best ideas in science are very, very simple. Einstein himself said of the theory: 'I succeeded because I have a beginner's mind.'

The reason why I now want to have a good simple look at relativity in the next section is because it started physics on its way to a view of the universe which makes the possible effects of mind on matter much easier to understand. It also showed that both space and time were changeable and not rigid absolutes.

4. Elastic Time and the Patent Clerk

Remote viewing experiments suggest that information can get across space in ways that Newtonian physicists would say was impossible.

However, in 1905 an engineer in a Swiss patent office created a theory which stood science on its head. Before his time, the world had been a tidy, mechanical place where everything happened in a tidy, predictable way. Space was the emptiness between things and time was an unvarying beat which remained exactly the same everywhere in the universe. Einstein's theory was called the Special Theory of Relativity, and it began physics on its way towards understanding the idea that mind can influence matter.

Let me tell you now that there is no reason *at all* why you should see that connection at present. What has space and time got to do with mind affecting matter or mind communicating with mind? *Nothing* in Newton's world but a *great deal* in the world of Einstein. We are entirely used to the commonsense notion that our bodies move around in an *empty* space and *fixed* time as told on our watches, and that this is the only reality.

There is obviously nothing wrong with that assumption in everyday life. We reach out across empty space to pick up a teacup, and the time on our watch tallies exactly enough with the time signal on the radio. Therefore, if minds can communicate across that sort of everyday space and everyday time, there is clearly something incomplete about this everyday way we look at space and time.

So it is important to understand how Einstein looked at space and time because it *is* related to those abilities. To him it was not just an empty *nothing* with isolated *things* in it. It was to do with *where* people make their observations from and what *time* it is where they are when they make the observations.

That is not at all obvious, however. In my living room I can see a friend from the *here* of my chair or the other side of the room or on television from Australia for that matter; it makes no difference to me; our watches keep the same time. Nevertheless there *is* a difference and it does *matter*.

One book about relativity stands out above all others for its stunning and simple lucidity. It was published in 1927. Who is it by? You've guessed: Albert Einstein. Nearly the whole book is about a train and an embankment. It's called *Relativity*, [1] and it is utterly and beautifully simple. I particularly like what he wrote in the Preface:

[1] A. Einstein, *Relativity*, Crown Publishers, New York, 1927

In the interests of clearness, it appeared to me that I should repeat myself frequently, without paying the slightest attention to the elegance of the presentation. I adhered scrupulously to the precept of that brilliant theoretical physicist, L. Boltzmann, according to whom matters of elegance ought to be left to the tailor and the cobbler. . . .

So I am going to use Einstein's own example because it is so simple and easy to understand.

Einstein retained a very simple approach to things. He was obsessed with the nature of reality, but he also had an elegantly logical mind, and so was not prepared to accept unquestioningly his view of the world about him as being either real or the same for everyone else. I knew an elderly German physicist who worked with him a little after his Special Theory was published. He told me that Einstein became obsessed with the word 'simultaneity' and went around grabbing people by the lapels and demanding to know what they meant by 'simultaneity'.

His basic thesis was that there is no such thing as a single, absolute reality. Here is how he showed it using a train. [With some trepidation, I have altered the account to make it even clearer for this book]:

Einstein imagined two observers, one standing inside a moving train at a window looking out, and the other sitting on the embankment watching the train move by, and the other observer at the window.

He made two rules for his experiment. First, that the train and the observer on it were moving past the observer on the embankment at a steady speed; second, that *neither* observer should be able to communicate with the other.

He then asked one very simple question: if the observer on the train dropped a ball out of the window, how would he see the ball change in shape, size and position, and how would the observer on the embankment see the ball change?

Let us start with what the observer on the train sees as he drops the ball out of the window. He sees a circle getting *smaller and smaller* and moving in a direction *opposite* to that of the train.

The observer on the embankment sees a circle which stays the *same size* moving in a curve in the *same direction* as the train. Both observers can film what they saw and both films will verify exactly what they claim they saw.

Fig. 21
Einstein's own example of the effect of relativity on ideas of reality is to imagine two observers, one on a train in steady motion, the other on the embankment watching the train go by. The observer on the train drops a large ball out of the window, and records what he sees: 'I saw a circular ball getting smaller and smaller and moving in a direction opposite to that of the train.'

The observer on the embankment watches the same event, and records: 'I saw a circular ball fall from the train, which remained the same size and moved in the same direction as the train.' Each observer records a separate reality.

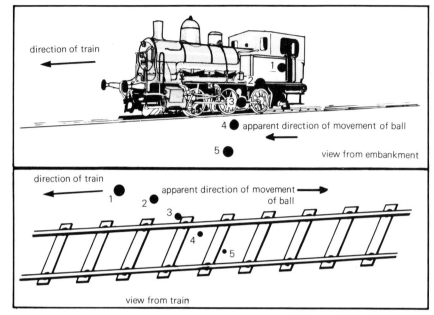

Now to the crunch. Each observer faithfully and accurately recorded an entirely *different* reality. Try it for yourself using a car, two observers and a beachball.

Well, there is obviously no problem about that in real life, because someone else looking at both observers can easily explain the differences between the two observations by telling them about the moving train. But if the third observer is asked what he saw, he will say something entirely *different* again from the other two observers. If a *fourth* observer was looking at the other three...

Suppose, however, that I am looking at a star, millions of light years away, through an astronomical telescope. Then I can *never* assume what I see out there to be true or real because there is no one else I can talk to *simultaneously* out there. Suppose I was looking at the Andromeda Galaxy with a telescope. It is millions of light years away, so I can never compare notes with an Andromedan *simultaneously* because of the *time* it takes for messages to go to and from Andromeda and Earth. (Do you remember watching the Moon shots? The delay was noticeable even then.)

In fact, if the Andromedans were looking at Earth *now* or the *now* by our watches they would be seeing stone age man because the light from the stone age has only just got there. We, too, are seeing Andromeda as it was thousands of years ago. So for all we know, it might have blown up and disappeared thousands of years ago by *our* time. Therefore reality does depend on *where* you are and *when* you are, and there can never be such a structure as an absolute single reality to which everything else is compared. This means that we are forced to look at connections and interactions across space and time in a more analytical way.

I've been talking about effects at enormous distances, and these make no real difference to us in everyday life. If I'm in the room with you, I know exactly where you are, and I know what time your watch is telling too, because I can see the watch and talk to you.

That is what our senses tell us. What Einstein demonstrated was that it is no good looking at space by itself or time by itself; instead we have to invent a something called *space-time*, because the two are always connected. So it is no use me looking at something which just happens in space or an event that just happens at a certain time. In fact, even in the short distance between us if we're in the same room, there is still a small loss of simultaneity. It's just that our senses cannot appreciate it.

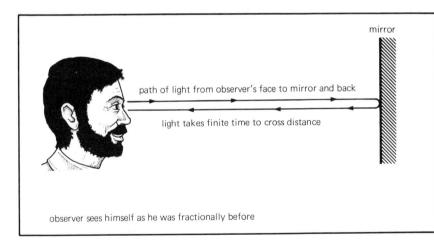

mirror

path of light from observer's face to mirror and back

light takes finite time to cross distance

observer sees himself as he was fractionally before

Fig. 22
Even in everyday life, there is no such thing as absolute simultaneity, as this example illustrates. When you look at yourself in a mirror, you do not see yourself as you are, but as you were an instant in the past: it takes light a small but finite time to travel to and from the mirror and your face.

As a matter of fact, no human has *ever* seen themselves as they *are* in a mirror. They have only seen themselves an instant in the past as they *were* when the light from their face travelled across space to reach the mirror and then was reflected to their eye and then on up their optic nerves to the brain. I can visualise space as just emptiness and I can visualise time as the sequence of ticks of my watch, but I *cannot visualise* space-time. It does not make sense and I can make no model of it in my head. Neither can anyone else including physicists. Do not get the idea that physicists are gifted with a special sight; they are not, they are just the same as you and I and everyone else in this respect. Space-time was a necessary invention because it helped to explain unknown events whether they could be visualised or not. One elderly don at Oxford said that he had spent much of his life trying to visualise space-time. After a lifetime of contemplation, he was asked on his death-bed if he had succeeded. 'Once or twice I caught a glimpse,' he replied.

So what does relativity do for our understanding of the universe? It fills in some really serious gaps in knowledge. If you want to read more about it there are other recent, simple accounts of its basic ideas. [2, 3] There are also a number of books and over-complicated television programmes which have made the whole idea thoroughly obscure and difficult.

Can it though be shown by *experiment* that relativity is a real, solid and useful idea? Yes, it can. An atomic clock keeps the best time on earth. It is accurate to one ten-millionth of a second per year and it is more accurate than the movement of the stars and the planets. In 1971, two physicists, Hefele and Keating, took four atomic clocks like the one in the picture and put two on one jet and two on another. One jet streaked round the earth in an easterly direction, the other in a westerly direction. When the two pairs of clocks were brought together again and compared in the same place, each pair told a different time. [4]

The really fascinating aspect of this experiment was that the mathematics of relativity theory predicted that the eastbound clocks would lose 40 billionths of a second; they actually lost 59. The theory predicted a gain of 275 billionths for the westbound clocks and they actually gained 273 billionths of a second. (The apparently great difference between 40 and 59 is, in fact, a remarkably good fit between theory and experiment in physics.)

The *only* piece of information I want you to take from this experiment is that *time* can be demonstrated to vary when the clock measuring it travels through *space*. Forget all other considerations for the moment.

Supposing we can agree that space and time always have to be linked in the new physics. Does that *explain* the paranormal? No. What it *does* do however, is to give us something to work with; it brings physics and the paranormal a little closer. The experiments of Targ and Puthoff show that some people have the ability to capture information across space, without using their normal

[2] G. Zukav, *The Dancing Wu Li Masters*, Rider Hutchinson, London, 1979; Fontana/Collins, London, 1980

[3] F. Capra, *The Tao of Physics*, Wildwood House, London, 1975; Fontana/Collins, London, 1976

[4] Quoted in N. Calder, *Einstein's Universe*, BBC Publications, London, 1976

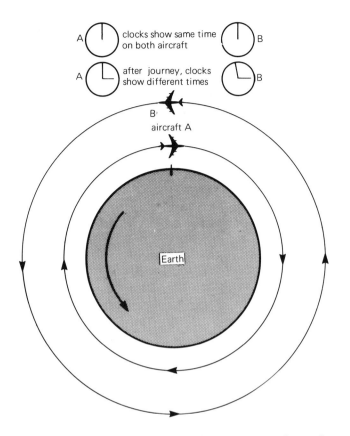

A ⊙ clocks show same time on both aircraft ⊙ B

A ⊙ after journey, clocks show different times ⊙ B

aircraft A

Earth

Fig. 23
Hefele and Keating tested the practical effects of relativity on space and time. Two jets were flown as fast as possible around the world in opposite directions. Each jet carried two atomic clocks, both pairs previously synchronised with each other; each told the same time when they left. When the jets returned to the point of departure, each pair of clocks told a different time. Motion through space has had an effect on time.

senses; now we can begin to look at this as not to do with *space* or *time* alone, but with *space-time*. Somehow the message has to get from sender to receiver; from the target location to the laboratory.

So now, armed with the basic idea of *space-time* instead of a real and absolute space, and a variable time between two regions of space instead of an absolute time, we can begin to see that the separation between two people in a remote viewing experiment is not quite such a clear-cut entity as it would have been to a Newtonian physicist.

What Einstein really showed is that: what happens in space and time can affect both space and time. Or, put another way: the deed can affect the nature of the universe.

Atomic clocks placed side by side on a bench continue to tell the *same* time. The deed was to put them side by side. Atomic clocks swung round the world in opposite directions on jets tell *different* times when they are brought together again. The deed was to swing them round the world.

In one magnificent and totally original inroad into the nature of the universe, Einstein showed that instead of a fixed, static, unchanging and mechanical universe, there was a shifting dynamic of change and interaction. The 'Universe of God the clockmaker' had been replaced by the 'Universe of God the cosmic dancer'.

Remote viewing could work in a number of ways. It could be that the minds of the outbound, remote, team connected directly with the mind of the inbound, laboratory subject, or it could be that the mind of the inbound person simply 'saw' by some paranormal means into the place where the outbound team went, the outbound team acting as some sort of beacon. Some investigators are even beginning to question whether the sender, receiver situation is necessary at all. In particular, the occurrence of 'displacement' results suggests that it may not be.

So far we have not progressed far enough to decide on any particular mechanism, and to help on the way towards one I now want to look at some experiments which have been done on the possibility of mind-to-mind communication. They are among the most reliable and repeatable experiments in the field of paranormal research, and they occur in the strange world of the *Ganzfeld*.

5. Mind Talk

Suppose two people try to communicate with their minds and one tries to send a mental signal to the other. Then like any radio signal, there could be some unwanted noise between the two, which gets in the way of clear transmission. Everyone has experience of this when they turn on a cheap radio; there is music, but there is also background hiss and crackle. Some experimenters have argued that the brain has to take in a lot of noise as well as signal and if the noise could be removed (like a 'Dolby' system on a hi-fi tape recorder), it might be easier to get sender and receiver to achieve successful communication with their minds because the channel between them was freed of some of the unwanted interference. Their brains would be quieter, and any potential paranormal channel might be cleared.

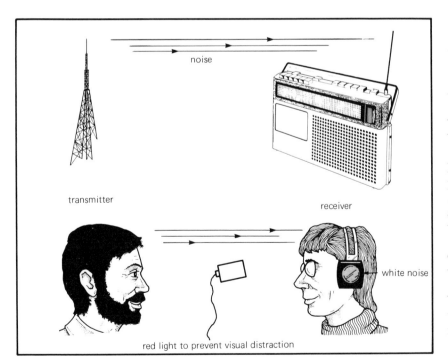

Fig. 24
In the Ganzfeld technique, the senses of the 'receiver' are shielded from unwanted signals by placing half ping-pong balls over the eyes, and bathing the subject in dim red light. His hearing is shielded by playing 'white noise' into earphones: it sounds like a distant waterfall. Reducing interference in Ganzfeld is analogous to reducing unwanted signals and static between a radio transmitter and receiver.

The conscious brain is actually in a constant tumult. The senses bombard it every second of the waking day with literally millions of signals from the eyes and ears alone, and if these could be shut down or made more even, some experimenters hold that it might give minds a better chance to communicate paranormally.

The technique is called Ganzfeld. 'Ganzfeld' is German meaning 'all field', and it means here an even surrounding field of information presented to the senses. This is basically how it is done (different experimental groups use different detailed versions of this method): two people are used as subjects; one acts as 'sender' and the other as 'receiver'; the aim is to see whether the receiver can identify the thoughts of the sender.

The 'receiver' is put in a room with half ping-pong balls taped over his eyes and a red light outside the ping-pong balls, so that all he can see is a dim diffuse pink background light with no images or pictures. He then dons earphones and listens to a recording of what is called 'white noise'. This is a soft mixture of all sound frequencies which adds up to no particular sound picture. It sounds very much like a distant waterfall.

In this way, say the experimenters, the mind of the 'receiver' is shielded from unnecessary signals, and, it is argued, the mind is freed and made more sensitive to any paranormal signals. In some experiments, the whole laboratory is also shielded by a wire mesh which is earthed and this is to prevent all the radio and television signals which are flying around space from getting into the mind of the 'receiver'.

Finally, an electrode is attached to the finger of the 'receiver' which connects to a recorder outside the shielded room. This shows the experimenter how relaxed the subject is. This part of the apparatus makes a measurement and recording of the electrical resistance on the skin, called the 'galvanic skin response' or g.s.r. The amount of skin sweat is an important factor here in determining the value of the g.s.r. The lower the trace, the more relaxed; the higher the trace, the less relaxed. The 'sender' in another room about twenty yards away is not shielded or subject to any shut-down of his senses, because the experimenters have discovered that the 'sending' process is more successful when the subject is alert and wakeful. In one experimental protocol, the sender is given four randomly selected words from a target pool of words and asked to form a 'thought picture' with them. The words are all linked to a single theme. For example, these four words were actually used in one experiment: 'fire', 'anvil', 'hammer', 'blacksmith'. The sender then tries to transmit the pictures he imagines from the words.

The 'receiver' then tries to imagine, visualise or see what the 'thought pictures' of the sender were. Finally, the descriptions made on the tape recorder by the receiver and the target words are sent to an independent judge, to see whether there has been a 'hit'. A 'hit' simply means that the receiver recorded something which was sufficiently similar to the target words to be identified. In one particular case, the receiver recorded the following words: 'I think I can see a fire and there is a hammer and an anvil...'

Most scientists who work in the paranormal agree that Ganzfeld experiments provide the most reliable and repeatable results in the whole field. One of the first people to use the technique was Charles Honorton, who works at the Maimonides Medical Center in Brooklyn, New York. Shortly after he had put a Ganzfeld laboratory together, he was visited by Ellen Messer, who was then a psychiatric nurse working at the Roosevelt Hospital in Manhattan. She had heard of Honorton's work and wanted to try an experiment with him, because she felt, from previous experiences of her own, that she might be successful.

Charles Honorton had already had some success with the method and published his results. [1] Then a producer from the National Film Board of Canada heard about the work and asked if he could make a film about it. Honorton agreed, provided that they filmed a real experiment and not a simulation, much as we did for the remote viewing experiment with Professor Rauscher in California.

[1] C. Honorton and S. Harper, *Journal of the American Society for Psychical Research*, vol. 68, 1974

Ellen Messer was the subject and she was put into a darkened room under Ganzfeld conditions; half ping-pong balls over the eyes, and white noise playing into earphones. She was in voice communication with one experimenter but with no one else. The experimenter was not in communication either with the other experimenter or with the sender, who was looking at a wheel of seven colour transparencies and trying to generate mental images about them to 'send' to Messer.

During the thirty-five minutes that elapsed she said on tape: 'I am floating over some sort of landscape. It's surrealistic. Watergate came to my mind. It's the name of a night club on 72nd Street. And marquees, night club marquees. Just seeing night club marquees in Las Vegas.'

After she had finished, she was handed duplicates of four colour transparency wheels, only one of which was the wheel the sender had been given to work with. She chose one, shouting, 'I can't believe it.' The wheel contained seven transparencies of buildings and nightclubs in Las Vegas. [2]

[2] N. Bowles, F. Hynds and J. Maxwell, *Psi Search*, Harper and Row, New York, 1978

Nevertheless, one experiment like that is nothing like enough to be able to say that 'sender' and 'receiver' were communicating paranormally. It could be luck or chance. Every so often, someone in the receiver room is going to hit on a picture of the target words by chance. The experimenter may have been encouraging both sender and receiver unconsciously.

So more questions have to be answered. Why is it not just a chance effect? The answer to this is that Ganzfeld work has now been carried out in about twenty-eight institutions, and published results show that identification between sender and receiver are sufficiently above chance to make this vanishingly unlikely.[3, 4, 5]

[3] L. and W. Brand, *Research in Parapsychology* (1975), Scarecrow Press, Metuchen, New Jersey, 1975

[4] M. York, *Research in Parapsychology* (1976), Scarecrow Press, Metuchen, New Jersey, 1976

[5] A. Stanford and A. Neylon, *Research in Parapsychology* (1974), Scarecrow Press, Metuchen, New Jersey, 1974

[6] C. Honorton, *Proceedings of Parapsychological Foundation* (1977), Paris, 1977

Honorton has calculated for example that his results combined with the results from ten other studies give positive results of one hundred billion to one over chance.[6]

I want now to return to the meaning of the word 'chance' again. Earlier, I used coin-tossing as an example.

Now consider a pack of 25 cards. There are 5 numbers only in the pack, the digits 1, 2, 3, 4 and 5. So there are 5 cards showing a 1, 5 showing a 2 and so on. I now shuffle the cards and start turning them over face up one by one. As I turn each one up, I press a buzzer which tells you in another room to make a guess as to which number was on the card.

Remember, 5 numbers occurring 5 times in a pack of 25 cards. If we perform one run of 25 guesses, by *chance* alone you should guess 5 cards correctly. If we try two runs of 25 guesses, by *chance* you should get 10 right. Three runs, 15 and so on. If you get a much larger number correct, there comes a point when the odds against that score occurring by chance – that is when no other factors are involved – become so large that *some* factor must be involved other than *chance*. This point is what statisticians call 'statistically significant'.

You may think that is a rather long-winded way of saying that the results were 'extremely odd'. Actually, it is more exact than that. Let us return to the cards. In one run of 25 you should get 5 right. If I calculate how many you would need to get right for the odds to be 20 to 1 against it would be 9 in one run. You might therefore think that in two runs of 25 you would need to get 18 right for the odds to be 20 to 1 against.

Actually it does not work quite like that and the 20 to 1 odds go like this:

Runs	Chance Score	Significant level for odds to be 20 to 1 against results being due to chance
1	5	9
2	10	16
3	15	22
4	20	28
5	25	34
10	50	63

You might still argue those mathematical levels have still been selected by the *opinion* of statisticians, and this to some extent is true. Nevertheless at least it is a mathematically informed opinion which is generally agreed upon by professionals (although a scientist who taught me once remarked: 'Statistics should only be legal between consenting adults'). There is another word we need to look at in relation to experiments on the paranormal. It is 'random'. Most people have an idea of what they mean by 'random'. If you throw a bucketful of marbles into the air, the pattern the marbles will make when they stop rolling on the ground and come to rest is likely to be random. That is to say, no one is likely to see recognisable shapes in the array of marbles. The problem with that idea is that they *may* make a pattern. They might look like a cross, or even one day come down looking exactly like your mother-in-law.

The word 'random', as used in statistics, means something different. If the marbles were made up of equal numbers of five different colours, and we put them in a barrel, seal it and roll it down a bumpy hill and then shake one marble out of the barrel, a statistician will say that the colour of the marble which comes out will be as near as you can get to a random choice. Actually statisticians believe that the word 'random' describes only what you *do* – making a random choice, for example – and does not describe some inherent property of the group of things you are examining. So we can make a random choice from a number of things, but this does not describe anything about the things. That is to say each of the five colours has an equal chance of emerging. However, even statisticians worry about the word, and so, for our purposes here, 'random' means something in which we can discover no order or sequence.

If we look at snowflakes in a blizzard, we can discover no order or sequence in the pattern they make, unless the wind blows. Then they will suddenly all shift in one direction; we can then see order, and their pattern is no longer random but ordered.

Disraeli wrote: 'There are lies, damned lies and statistics', but they *are* the best way we have of analysing events. Let's return to the evaluation of Ganzfeld experiments.

Charles Honorton's work shows that the odds against all the Ganzfeld results he studied occurring by chance alone were so great that other factors must have been involved. What could these factors have been? Were the judges of the similarity between the receiver's comments and the chosen pictures independent? Did the experimenters give either 'sender' or 'receiver' any conscious or unconscious cues or clues? What are the opportunities for cheating? How random is the selection of the target words or pictures from the target pool?

As a matter of fact these questions have been answered time and again in the literature on Ganzfeld experiments, but in the same way as we put ourselves into a remote viewing experiment in California, we decided it would be useful if I was put into a Ganzfeld experiment to experience the situation for myself. If, indeed, there was anything like faulty experiment or fraud, both Richard Mervyn, the Producer, and myself and the camera crew would have to be involved. The results of the experiments shook me to the core.

Dr Carl Sargent does experiments using the Ganzfeld technique at the psychology laboratories at Cambridge University, and his doctorate is the first in Cambridge to be awarded for studies in parapsychology. We arranged for me to be the 'receiver' subject in a Ganzfeld experiment, with his colleague Trevor Harley as 'sender'. Once again, we made a film of the experiment, but this time we worked slightly differently to the technique we used in recording the remote viewing experiment.

Since the 'receiver', that is to say, me, had to be in Ganzfeld conditions, and this means that my surroundings had to be relaxed and quiet, we judged it to be impossible to film in real time, since the lights and bustle of a television crew in full flight would inevitably generate conditions of anxiety and tension. So this is what we did:

First of all, Carl Sargent selected the pictures for Trevor Harley to use as sender. There is a target pool of about forty sets of four sealed envelopes, each one separately coded for its set on the outside. Each set is of four different pictures. A computer selects one of the code numbers, and the four sealed envelopes with the set code number on it are taken from the pool and held sealed by Carl Sargent. The code number is known to him and this enables him to select duplicates of the pictures inside the sealed envelopes. The code number was unknown to me and unknown to the sender, Trevor Harley.

One other feature of this target selection process must be mentioned. When an experiment has been completed, the subject's name and the code number on the envelope are written down

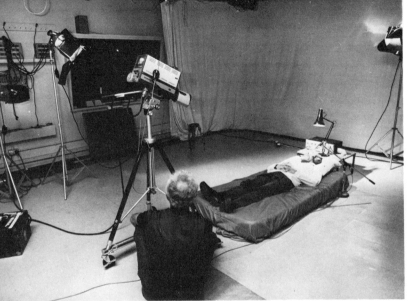

Fig. 25
The Cambridge laboratory in which Dr Carl Sargent carries out the Ganzfeld experiments. Kit Pedler is lying on the mattress, wearing headphones through which white noise is played, his eyes covered by half ping-pong balls, and bathed in red light. He is observed by a video camera.

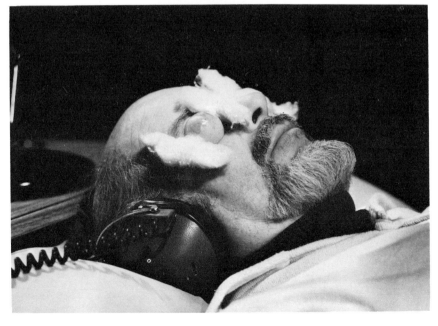

Fig. 26
A close-up of the precautions taken to ensure that the subject in a Ganzfeld experiment has no visual distractions.

together. If that subject does a second experiment, the envelopes with that code number are removed from the target pool, to guard against the real possibility that a particular subject could develop a good memory for particular pictures he had already seen. Once Carl Sargent has the sealed envelopes and the duplicates of the pictures inside it, he keeps the duplicates and hands the sealed envelopes to Trevor Harley.

Trevor Harley then synchronises his watch with Carl Sargent's watch and leaves the room with the four still sealed envelopes; one only to be opened. The producer of the series noted that the envelopes were in fact still sealed when he did so, and that he did not look at the duplicates; neither did Carl Sargent.

I was, at this time already lying down in the laboratory and had sealed the ping-pong balls over my eyes and adjusted the ear-phones playing 'white noise'. Carl then came in and chatted for a while and asked me to adjust the volume level of the white noise to a comfortable level, positioned the microphone into which I was going to record my thoughts, and left the room. The experimental period of thirty minutes then began.

My thoughts were mixed. All I was initially aware of was the red light flooding my field of vision through the ping-pong balls and the soft waterfall sound of the white noise in my ears. For some reason, I became anxious and tense. Looking back on the occasion I think it was due to the different parts of my mind working against each other.

Part of me was saying, 'What rubbish you've got yourself into Kit'; another part was saying, 'Go on, you know you can do it if you want to; your rational mind accepts the evidence, so why don't you just settle down and get on with it.' Yet another part was saying, 'My God, what if I succeed. I don't want to be a psychic!'

After a few minutes I managed to get the warring factions of my divided self under better control and settled down to 'looking out' into the red light. It was a soothing thing to do. I knew I was being looked at like an experimental animal through the thick glass which separated the recording area from the laboratory, but that no longer seemed to matter.

Stiffly at first, and then more easily, I began to talk into the microphone. Having listened repeatedly to the playback of what I said at the time, it is clear that my mood and demeanour had changed. Normally I talk fast and in a staccato manner. On the recording, I used words very slowly and with greater care. A physiologist would have said that 'my level of arousal was lower'; that probably says little more than 'I was relaxed'.

Then I began to imagine pictures, and to conjure them into the red light; vague shapes began to swirl into view, stay for a few seconds and then dismantle themselves into what seemed to be a randomly moving background. Then I realised I was thinking at the same time. I was *trying* to create the images myself as if to say: I wonder if that is what (he) the sender is looking at. I found, in short, that I was determined to succeed. After a while I managed to cut intellectualisations like that out of my mind and began instead to de-focus everything I was aware of into the red light. What seemed a long time later, my mind was finally quiet; anxiety had receded, and I lay quite relaxed, waiting.

It is very difficult to describe the pictures that came into my mind, even though I spent twelve years of my life studying the eye and vision. They were half way between actual images, mind pictures and language description and they were tucked away in part of my mind which I had not previously been aware of.

For the next thirty minutes, I lay quietly, reporting the images through the microphone; then there were voices, the lights came on and the experiment was over. Immediately I had adjusted to the light, Carl Sargent took me over to a table; we sat down and he spread the four duplicate pictures out in front of me.

He then explained the judging process. What follows now is an actual transcript of the tape recording of Carl explaining and beginning the judging of the four pictures with me. Reproductions of the four pictures are in Figs. 27–30.

CS Okay. *A*, picture *B*, picture *C*, and *D*. Now, off the top of your head, which of these four do you think it might be?

KP: That one. [Fig. 28]

CS: Right. Okay. Now, what we're going to do is that we're going to go through it in more detail, we're going to check every single thing that you said individually and score it against the four different pictures, giving each thing a score between nought and ten. So a score of nought means what you said, what you saw, doesn't relate to this picture at all. Whereas a score of ten means it's absolutely perfect, that the picture is exactly what you've seen. And things in between where there's a bit of correspondence is a score between nought and ten. Okay?

KP: Okay.

CS: Well, we'll try it and see how it goes. The first thing you say is, 'I see grey circles with a darker surround.' Now which of the pictures – and there may be none at all, there may be more

Figs. 27–30
The four pictures used
in the Ganzfeld
experiment performed
for the series. Picture
A (Fig. 27) was the one
selected for the target,
but picture C (Fig. 29)
was the one to which
Kit Pedler achieved the
closest description.
Out of 10 completed
studies with 306
sessions, Carl Sargent
reports 118 direct hits.
The chance of this
result happening by
chance alone is less
than one in half a
million.

than one – do you think might have that thing in it or something like it?

KP: Well, nothing there.

CS: Okay.

KP: Nothing there.... But there are some grey circles there so –
they're not really what I saw so I'll give them maybe two.

CS: Okay.

KP: And over here, well, just, but, you know, one.

CS: Right. Okay. Well, the second thing you see is bars and grilles;
they're light grey with a dark grey surround against the red.
Okay...

The procedure went on point by point like this for some ten
minutes and then we came to the summing up.

CS: Okay, well, I've added up the scores for the first four pictures!
28 points, 61 points, 2 points, 37 points. So it looks as though
you've got an obvious first choice and sort of obvious fourth,
and two in the middle. So, how would you put them in order?

KP: Well, I've no doubt that that one is top. (Fig. 28)

CS: Yes.

KP: But as between – and that one's bottom, incidentally. (Fig. 30)
I find nothing there at all.

CS: Okay.

KP: Between these two ... I think that one second. (Fig. 27)

CS: Okay. Right now we'll have Trevor summoned.

KP: Right.

Some minutes later sender Trevor Harley came into the room
carrying the picture, the opened envelope and the sketches he had
made around the subject of the picture during the sending period.
He spaced them out on the table:

TH: Well, it's this one, A.

KP: Ah. Well, I'll be blowed.

CS: Well, your intuition to put that second rather than third was
certainly right.

KP: Yes, but I didn't put it first.

CS: No, you didn't put it first, but nonetheless there are some interesting points about putting that second in this case.

There were. After the judging process of the actual experiment was finished, the film crew arrived and we recreated the whole experiment on film, but it was not just a simulation. What we did was to use the actual verbal transcript which we had just recorded during the experiment and create television images around it as accurately as possible.

This was the best we could do in the circumstances, because of the need for complete relaxation on the part of myself the receiver, and because of the inevitable noise and bustle which goes with film-making.

Studying my transcript and the pictures, the results are extraordinary. Here is a piece of the transcript of my voice:

—And on the left, on the left is —a black saw-tooth pattern like one of those old wood saws...
— Okay, yes slopes. All triangular slopes pointing upwards with vertical spikes.
— The — yes — all slopes, vertical slopes with their points facing upwards.
—It's a roof line, viewed from slightly above. Village roof lines and chimneys.

This repetitive reference seems to fit the black triangular peaks of the witches' hats very well, but I did *not* rank that picture top. Here is more transcript:

There are palm trees, half way up a mountain in silhouette.

As you can see in the fantasy by Robert Dean, there are palm-like trees half way up a mountain in silhouette.

Nevertheless this is the picture I ranked first but *not* the one sender Trevor Harley had selected. Nevertheless, the correspondence between the transcript of what I said and the actual picture is extraordinary. There are indeed palm-like trees, they are half way up a mountain in silhouette. Four linked properties in one picture.

So the question has to be asked: Is it possible to calculate the odds of this correspondence occurring by chance? I asked Carl Sargent. He replied that it was not possible to calculate numerical odds (how many possible different pictures are there?), but that it was *very* unlikely.

It is also interesting that the references by me to 'black saw-tooth patterns like one of those old wood saws' and 'triangular slopes pointing upwards', and 'slopes, vertical slopes' and 'roof lines' not only fit the row of pointed hats in the picture I ranked second, but they also fit the mountain outlines in the Dean fantasy; but less well.

The final point of great interest was that the 'fit' of my verbal transcript and the pictures was measurably better during the second half of the thirty-minute experimental period. The measurement technique used by Dr Sargent is an orthodox scoring method used by experimental psychologists: and, unknown to me, Trevor Harley only started opening the envelope and attempting to send during the *second* half of the thirty-minute period.

It is a complicated result. In conversation with Carl Sargent, we agreed that this is a good 'hit'; there was once again displacement, as we found in the remote viewing experiment.

Much later, I asked Professor Rauscher what she thought of this result and without any hesitation at all, she retorted: 'That's because you didn't want to get the right one right did you?' This is much nearer the mark than anything else. Liz Rauscher is highly intuitive about people and the anxiety and mental confusion I felt at the beginning of the experiment was at the heart of the matter; half of me wanted to succeed and half wanted to fail.

Some subjects who act as 'receiver' in Ganzfeld experiments have extraordinary and regular successes. In a later section I shall be looking at the relationship of personality to extra-sensory abilities since the mental attitudes of personality type seem to be centrally important to abilities in situations like Ganzfeld experiments.

One of Carl Sargent's subjects who regularly achieves good results started one experiment, then took off the ping-pong balls and the earphones and said into the microphone: 'There's no need to go any further, it's Blake's "Creation".' The picture selected by the 'sender' was indeed a reproduction of Blake's 'Creation'.

In conversation after the experiment I brought up the inevitable question of fraud and collusion and one of Carl Sargent's responses was, to me, very illuminating. He said this: 'There is only one way I can continue to do this work with any confidence at all, and that is by making my own experimental design as tight and foolproof as I can make it.'

This was the approach of any straightforward professional scientist, and I respect it entirely. There is now a mass of published experimental work using the Ganzfeld technique. Some of the experimental methods differ slightly in detail, but all use the basic procedure of shielding the mind of the receiver by shutting off unwanted auditory and visual noise.

I feel it is just worth mentioning that if anyone would like to accuse me of some sort of collusion with Carl Sargent during this experiment, they are welcome to do so, but they should make it eyeball to eyeball and I will promise them a brisk discussion!

It may be that, when a firmer theoretical basis for the paranormal emerges, both remote viewing and Ganzfeld results may turn out to be essentially the same phenomenon in slightly different guise but both suggest that information can cross space between minds and as we will see later on, information may turn out to be the basic commodity of the physicists' universe. Not atoms, protons, electrons or radiation, but just information.

So what has remote viewing and the Ganzfeld work got to do with the space-time of Einstein's world? What Einstein showed us is that there is no single or universal reality. In the train experiment, one observer existed in one reality, and the other existed in another and *both* were real, to the senses of both. The real problem that Einstein's work created was that his universe was completely contrary to our commonsense view of the universe. We cannot visualise space-time, and none of our senses can make any picture of it; it does explain more unknowns about the universe than if we assumed things to be as our senses do see them and so it had to be accepted. This was one of the most important turning points which lead from the old to the new physics.

In Newton's commonsense universe, the idea of two minds communicating across space was absolutely impossible, but the new physics was beginning to suggest that two objects or minds which appear to be separate to our senses may only have a space-*like* separation in space-time. But our senses tell us very clearly indeed that there *are* reliable spaces between objects, and that there really is a separation between the skin of our fingertips and something that we touch. 'Really is' is the problem: our senses tell us so, but the physics of Einstein and the scientists who came after him says otherwise.

There are many other experiments in physics like the one with the atomic clocks and the two jets which show quite conclusively that space and time vary according to *where* and *when* you are.

In 1908 Minkowski, a mathematician much revered by Einstein, wrote: 'Henceforth space by itself and time by itself are doomed to fade away into mere shadows, and only a kind of union of the two will preserve an independent reality.' [7]

[7] A. Lorens, A. Einstein, H. Minkowski and H. Weyle, *Principles of Relativity*, Dover, New York, 1952

There is one fable in physics which reinforces this statement in a rather attractive way: it is called the twin paradox. Two identical twins decide to become astronauts. One twin sets off from earth in a spaceship; the other stays at mission control. The twin on the spacecraft agrees to send a radio signal back to the twin at mission control every ten minutes. On board the spaceship, it is perfectly clear that that is what is happening. Every ten minutes according to the clock on board, he presses the button.

Fig. 31
The 'twin paradox' asks you to consider a pair of twins. One remains on earth at mission control; the other parks a spaceship in space. The twin on board the spaceship has previously agreed that he will send signals every ten minutes to the twin at mission control. In this situation, the twin in space observes that signals do leave his ship every ten minutes, and the twin at mission control agrees that the signals are arriving every ten minutes. The twin on the ship then accelerates away from the earth until he has reached nearly the speed of light. He is still sending signals every ten minutes. He is confident that the time between signals is indeed ten minutes. But the twin on earth now begins to receive signals at longer and longer intervals. To the twin left on earth, the time of the twin in space begins to slow down. The astronaut ages more slowly (in 'earth time'), and may return to earth to find his identical twin an old man while he is still young.

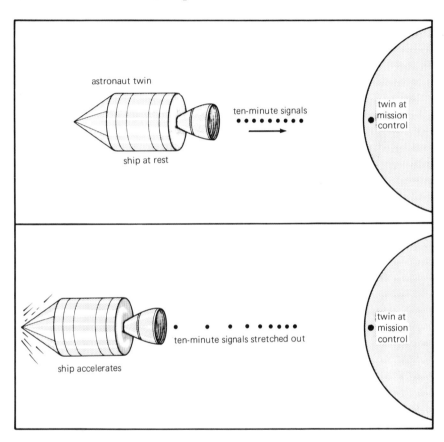

On earth, however, as the other twin watches the spaceship moving faster and faster until, when it is travelling at, say, two-thirds of the speed of light, he sees the ten-minute signals arriving at longer and longer intervals. Why? Because the ten-minute intervals are *stretched out* by the accelerating progress of the spaceship towards the speed of light.

The consequences of this situation, which physicists call the 'twin paradox', are quite awe-inspiring, because the twin on board will therefore age *less* than the twin at mission control. If both were twenty-five years old when they parted company and if the

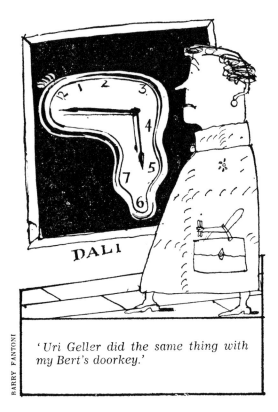

Fig. 32
A Barry Fantoni
cartoon from *The
Listener*, published at
the time of a Salvador
Dali exhibition.
Perhaps there is a
relation between all
the different
manifestations of 'psi'?

BARRY FANTONI

'*Uri Geller did the same thing with
my Bert's doorkey.*'

twin on the spaceship stayed away for two years, he might arrive
back at mission control twenty-seven years old only to find his
identical twin to be an old man of seventy.

This view of things reinforces the view that time is an elastic
quality. When we say that someone has a *premonition*, that is to
say they saw something *ahead* in time, it is no longer such an
obviously impossible claim. Although I have promised to stick to
accounts of experiments in the paranormal, there are other pre-
monitions to do with time which are not experiments, but which
are well documented and truly remarkable.

I have already described the extraordinary similarity between
the fictional SS *Titan*, and the factual SS *Titanic*, and that the
fictional ship was documented some twelve years before the real
ship was launched. Now look at the following passage:

*They have likewise discovered two lesser stars, or satellites [sic],
which revolve about Mars, whereof the innermost is distant from
the centre of the primary planet, exactly three of diameters, and
the outermost five; the former revolves in the space of ten hours
and the latter in twenty-one and a half.*

This is a passage from *Gulliver's Travels* written in 1726. 151 years later, two satellites were actually discovered circling Mars. The first is 1·5 Mars diameters away from the planet, the second 3·5 diameters. The orbit time of one is 7 hours 39 minutes and the second 30 hours 18 minutes. They are now well known as 'Phobos' and 'Deimos' and have been fully photographed by the deep-space probes.

Was it really coincidence that an author imagined and documented these two satellites with similar orbital diameters and orbital times a century and a half before they were actually discovered? As I pointed out in the case of the *Titanic*, we can never be absolutely sure, but there are several impressive correlations here. However, the length of time between record and event is long.

If physics now tells us that time and space are elastic and changeable qualities, then have any experiments in precognition or premonition been done which show measurable consistency? Do such tests show that the sensitivities of the human mind can exploit these elastic and changeable properties of time?

6. The Clock that Drooped

Dr Helmudt Schmidt was until 1967 a senior research physicist at the Boeing aircraft research laboratories – not a job in which bad experiment is likely to prevail for long. He became interested in premonition, but didn't call it by that name. He calls it 'precognition'. That only means 'to know something before it happens'.

He decided to experiment on it in this way. First, find something in nature which has no order to it all, something which behaves in a completely unpredictable or completely random way. (See page 57 for definition of 'random'. Every event the something produces has an equal chance of happening.) Then see if it is possible for someone to predict what happens.

First, he took a piece of radioactive material – he used Strontium 90. When radioactive material decays it does so on a random basis. Every time one atom in it decays, it fires out a high-speed particle, and the arrival of the particle can be recorded with the Geiger counter – a Geiger counter counts ionising particles and thus the amount of radioactivity. If the Geiger counter was kept running for a week, you could get a good idea of how many atoms were going to decay, but what you could never tell is the exact time the next atom was actually going to decay; in much the same way you could count the drips from a tap over a week, but never know exactly when the next drip will fall off. The intervals between decay particles arriving are absolutely random, and nobody can tell exactly when they are going to arrive.

Consider a small electronic box with four lights in a row and a button opposite each light. Helmudt Schmidt built a machine, driven by a radioactive source like Strontium. A circuit selects one light out of the four in the sequence 1, 2, 3, 4, 1, 2, 3, 4, several million times every second, but none of the lights goes on until one of the four buttons is pressed. The next particle which shoots out from a decaying atom stops the machine at whatever light is next going to be lit in the sequence 1, 2, 3, 4. When the machine stops, only then does the light come on.

Now, the subject is asked to predict which light is going to light

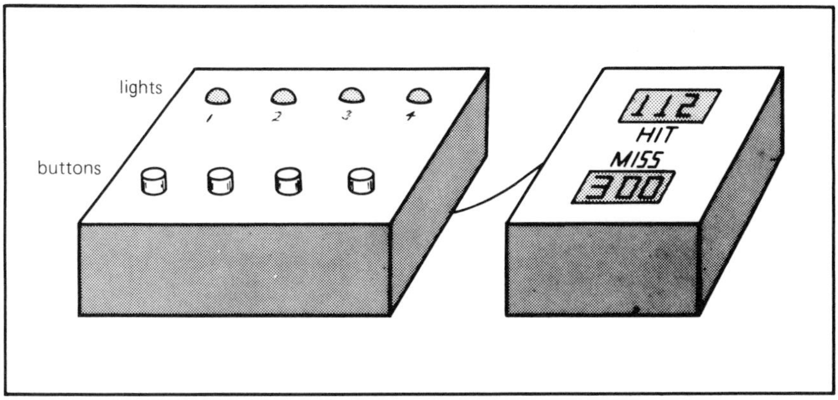

Fig. 33
Dr Helmudt Schmidt
built this machine to
test precognition. Four
lights are lit at random
– the random source is
radioactivity. Opposite
each light is a button;
the subject is asked to
press the button
opposite the light
which will come on
next. If he predicts the
light correctly, the
machine records a
'hit'; if he fails, a
'miss'.

up next; he presses the button next to the light he chooses. If that light goes on, he is right and the machine scores a 'hit'. If he is wrong, the machine scores a 'miss'. With four lights, you would expect everyone to get about one in four guesses correct over a long period.

So, if anyone could get well above one in four over a long period, then that could be interpreted as precognition or knowing which light was going to light ahead of time. But before we reach that conclusion there are more questions to answer.

Could there have been human errors in the recording? All Dr Schmidt's machines which I have personally examined have automatic and error-free recording systems based upon fail-safe electronics.

Again, could there have been fraud or collusion? Dr Schmidt's experiments extend over a ten-year period, and have involved a very large number of people using machines which are sealed and tamper-proof. Unless someone is going to assume a collective fraud of that magnitude and duration, the results can really only be criticised on a statistical basis, and no one has done this successfully.

Again we have to return to ideas like chance, randomness and odds to get some idea of the significance of Dr Schmidt's results. What do they show?

In early experiments, Dr Schmidt worked with a subject who was also a physicist. In 7,600 trials, he achieved a success rate of 33·7 per cent where the chance expectancy was 25 per cent. The odds here against chance producing the result are about 100,000 to 1 against. In 63,000 trials of three subjects which followed, a success rate of 26·1 per cent resulted, where 25 per cent was expected by chance. The difference here is small, but the large number of trials increases the validity of the difference to a level where the odds against that happening by chance are in excess of 4,500,000,000 to 1 against. In 20,000 trials of other subjects, similar results were obtained. But then something entirely new appeared.

Some people did *consistently well* and others did *consistently badly*. That is to say some people could achieve a higher-than-chance result and other people could get lower-than-chance results (both of which, of course, are equally significant statistically).

In the chapter entitled 'Sheep and Goats' I will discuss this in more detail and show that these abilities are strongly related to the personality and attitudes of the people involved. The two groups are known to experimenters working in the field as 'psi-hitters' and 'psi-missers'.

Subsequent experimenters have confirmed that 'psi-missing' is a reliable phenomenon and just as significant as 'psi-hitting'. The plot thickens. Now I am sorry to have to tell you that it thickens again. If we look back over the 'protocol' of Dr Schmidt's experiments, they show that some people can achieve a precognitive view of what is going to happen in the future of a randomly driven machine. What does this mean?

Let's say at this stage that Dr Schmidt's experiments show a good valid connection between the machine and the mind of the subject, but we now need to get that connection clear. Psychologists talk about the 'cognitive abilities' of a subject, but they have not the slightest idea how to define this phrase precisely: so I shall not use it. It is only to do with the faculty of knowing. People working on the paranormal try to clarify what they observe. So they talk about four main types of paranormal activity.

1 *Precognition*: the mind crossing time.
2 *Telepathy*: the mind crossing distance.
3 *Clairvoyance*: the mind seeing things out of sight.
4 *Psychokinesis*: The mind affecting matter.

The *Oxford Dictionary* defines these as:

1 Foreknowledge.
2 Communication from one mind to another at a distance other than through the main senses.
3 Faculty of seeing mentally what is happening or exists out of sight.
4 The movement of physical objects by mental influence without physical contact.

Each description is a small masterpiece of unbiased description. If Dr Schmidt's successful subjects established some sort of connection or interaction with the machine then they could either be seeing ahead in time and this would be *precognition*, or they could be affecting the machine directly with their minds and this would be *psychokinesis*. So he carried out a detailed series of experiments to distinguish between these two possibilities.

In his earlier work Dr Schmidt had used a radioactive random source to work the lights, so if a subject got results above chance it could be that either the subject was seeing ahead of time with his mind (precognition); or that his mind was directly influencing some part of the machine itself (psychokinesis) – that is to say, the subjects were somehow reaching into the machine with their minds and either affecting the electronics or the random behaviour of the radioactive source. He therefore substituted the random source with a punched paper tape containing over 100,000 random digits – so that the output of the machine to the lights, and thus the sequence of lights, was already fixed and could not be influenced by the mind of the subject. This ruled out psychokinesis. Altogether he did 15,000 trials; some subjects got results above their expected chance level with odds of about 3,000,000 to 1 against.

This showed that the results were not produced by psychokinesis, because the operation of the lights was already under the control of fixed holes in a punch tape. The only way the subjects could have influenced the machine by psychokinesis would have been for their minds to punch new holes in the tapes, and this did not occur.

The possibility that the results could have been achieved by clairvoyance could not be ruled out, and Dr Schmidt also thought that psychokinesis could not be ruled out in some other part of the machine. Consequently he constructed an entirely different device to see whether subjects could use psychokinesis or 'mind over matter', to influence hardware. This is what he did.

First he constructed an electronic circuit which would give one of two results on a random basis. We have already looked at coin tossing and agreed that heads or tails will come down randomly, but over a long period, there will be 50 per cent heads and 50 per cent tails recorded. 'Heads' or 'tails' are both equally probably results on each toss of the coin. This is the same process; one of two results on a random basis. His circuit was called an *electronic coin tosser* for this reason.

Dr Schmidt then connected the electronic coin tosser to nine lights arranged in a circle. At the beginning of a run the light at

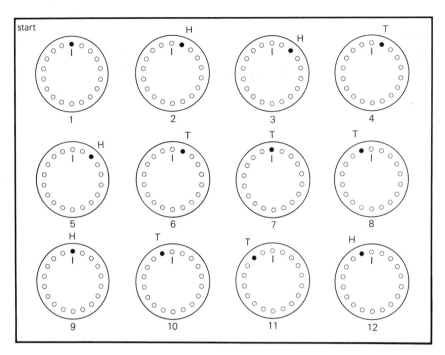

Fig. 34
Another of Dr
Schmidt's experiments
involves an electronic
coin tosser. Random
'heads' or 'tails' signals
make the light move
respectively clockwise
or anti-clockwise, one
step for each signal.
The lights therefore
fluctuate around top
centre. Some subjects
are able to influence
the lights to move
more in one direction
than the other.

twelve o'clock was lit. If 'heads' was injected into the light circuit
the next light anticlockwise was lit and if another 'heads', the next
light anticlockwise and so on. If 'tails' was called the next light
clockwise was lit. If another 'heads' was called the next light
clockwise lit, and so on.

In this way, the lights moved randomly clockwise and anti-
clockwise; the object was to discover whether a subject could
move the lights more in one direction or another in a non-random
or paranormal way over the odds expected by chance. Internal
electronic scoring devices were added to make the whole device
self-sufficient and tamper-proof in one box.

Left to itself and assuming the electronic coin tosser to be
properly random, the number of times the lights moved clockwise
and the number of times the lights moved anticlockwise should be
50:50. This turned out to be the case in a long series of blank
control experiments Dr Schmidt did to establish the reliability of
the machine. He also reversed the wire containing the 'heads'
signal with the wire containing the 'tails' signal to make sure that
the electronic coin tosser did not have some inbuilt biases. None
was found.

He worked with two groups of people: known 'psi-hitters' and
known 'psi-missers'. Altogether, after 32,768 trials, he found that
'hitters' moved the lights a significantly larger number of times

than 'missers' who moved the lights a significantly smaller number of times, with odds of 1,000 to 1 against chance alone being responsible in each case.

For example, a known 'hitter' achieved 52·5 per cent (2·5 per cent above chance) in 6,400 trials, whereas a known 'misser' achieved 47·75 per cent below chance in the same number of trials (2·25 per cent below chance). These departures from chance look small, but the odds against the difference between the two scores occurring by chance is about 10,000,000 to 1 against.

Dr Schmidt's work is probably the most copious and carefully performed research in the whole field of the paranormal, and other researchers are now achieving similar results. [1, 2, 3]

Dr Schmidt himself has also published many accounts of his work. [4]

Let us summarise so far. There is good evidence to show that some people can apparently predict a future event, and that others can affect electronic apparatus with their minds.

Helmudt Schmidt is a careful and methodical man. He dislikes quick, superficial conversation, and weighs his words with considerable care. He is also a highly experienced physicist who spent a considerable part of his life working on aspects of aircraft safety. After examining his apparatus and talking with him, I asked him how he felt about the apparent conflict between physics and the paranormal. He answered:

In physics we are always on the look out for something new, something which doesn't fit in, and I think that parapsychology is the prime candidate. If things really don't fit into the framework of physics, but seem to tell us there is something different there, we have to look at them.

Physics has been extremely successful so far and we can say that it has proved itself by now. I would say it is not surprising that these things happen. There seem to be some phenomena which physicists really have overlooked so far. Now, when we talk about the mind, then some physicists say that's not our realm, but I think that at some stage it is something we have to face. And it seems that these parapsychological questions provide a bridge from pure physics as we know it presently to the question of the mind. In parapsychology we know we can do experiments, and that is so pleasant for a physicist, because he can do something more than just think and philosophise.

I then asked him how he viewed the strange possibility that his work showed some sort of slip in time. He replied:

[1] E. Andre, *Journal of Parapsychology*, vol. 36, 1972

[2] C. Honorton and W. Barksdale, *Journal of the American Society for Psychical Research*, vol. 66, 1972

[3] R. Stanford et al., *Journal of the American Society for Psychical Research*, vol. 69, 1975

[4] H. Schmidt, *Journal of Applied Physics*, vol. 41, 1970; *Journal of the American Society for Psychical Research*, vol. 69, 1975; vol. 70, 1976; *Journal of Parapsychology*, vol. 33, 1969; vol. 37, 1973; vol. 38, 1974; *New Scientist*, vol. 44, 1969; vol. 49, 1971

It seems for me reasonable to look at the most unusual phenomena because that's probably where you can learn most, and there it seems that precognition is a good candidate. You look into the future and know something you shouldn't be able to know, and so either your mind probes into the future or, as I prefer to see it, future events cast a shadow back into the present; [my emphasis] what happens in the future affects my mind at this very moment; somehow there is a direct coupling between future and mind.

[5] H. Schmidt in C. Tart, H. Puthoff and R. Targ (eds.), *Mind at Large*, Praeger Scientific, New York, 1979

Dr Schmidt has now made a further analysis of his work [5] in which he is beginning to look at precognition as if part of the universe around us works in what physicists call a *non-causal* way.

This has a simple but very strange meaning. If I hit a ball with a bat, the *ball* was *caused* to move because the bat hit it and the *effect* was that the ball moved. It is obvious therefore that cause and effect rules much of our everyday life.

A non-causal universe is one where one event does not necessarily cause another but is simply *connected* to it; bat and ball simply show evidence of collision with each other: or, they *connect*. As we get further into some more of the ideas in the new physics, we will see that *connections* become more important than the one-way arrows of cause and effect. This makes better sense of Dr Schmidt's view of things: that future events can cast a shadow back into the present.

So far we have looked at what variable space-time means to the way we look at the world about us, and there we also found that all that observers can discover is what happens in their own vicinity; there are two realities, one for each observer. Neither one can discover anything absolute about the two together. All they can talk about are *connections* and interaction between them.

Physicists often talk about the vicinity around a something as its 'frame of reference'. This is a useful description because it creates a good visual picture; a box around the something. In the train experiment one observer was in the *frame of reference* of the train, and the other was in the *frame of reference* of the embankment. I shall return to this point again and again; it is crucial. Sir James Jeans, physicist, put it succinctly: 'As the new physics has shown, all earlier systems of physics, from the Newtonian mechanics down to the old quantum theory, fell into the error of identifying appearance with reality.' [6]

[6] J. Jeans, *The Mysterious Universe*, Cambridge University Press, 1930

At that point I should explain the terms 'quantum theory' and 'quantum mechanics'. *'Quantum theory'* is theoretical physics that assumes energy and radiation to be in the form of packets and 'quantum mechanics' is a method of analysing the universe making that assumption.

Where the concept helps in understanding paranormal happenings is that it sharply modifies the idea that we can *observe* anything. All we appear to be able to do is to *participate*, *interact* and *connect*.

Erwin Schrödinger, one of the founders of the new physics and one of the originators of quantum mechanics commented: 'Subject and object are only one. The barrier between them cannot be said to have broken down as a result of recent experiments in the physical sciences, for *this barrier does not exist.*' [7]

If we cannot really *observe*, but only participate, this is in complete conflict with our experience of everyday life. We *do* make absolute observation; we *do* reach out to pick up the tea-cup, and the assumption that the tea-cup is *out there* and that we are *in here* is completely reliable. Why do we need to talk about such strange and unlikely ideas?

We live everyday life much like a secret agent; we operate on the 'need-to-know' principle. Just as an agent is only told what he 'needs to know' about a particular intelligence situation, so do we find our way about the ordinary, three-dimensional, hard-edged world with a minimum of necessary need-to-know information; a scientist cannot leave *anything* unconsidered in trying to discover how something works. If there is a discrepancy in a series of

[7] E. Schrödinger, *What is Life and Mind and Matter?*, Cambridge University Press, 1955

Fig. 35
Werner Heisenberg, originator of the Uncertainty Principle.

observations, that discrepancy simply has to be included in any theory. It cannot be ignored without trying to see what gave rise to it. To operate the need-to-know principle in science would be to hide away from difficulties. So it was not wilfulness or the urge to be clever that made the new physicists think in this way; it was the enormous difficulties they had with the discrepancies, the properties of the universe they could not explain and which would not fit their view of how things work. One of the originators of the new physics, Werner Heisenberg, had an all-night discussion with another, Niels Bohr, and what they concluded so shocked them that Heisenberg rushed out to walk in a nearby park having exclaimed: 'I simply cannot believe that the universe is as *absurd* as it seems to be.'

They were forced to abandon their commonsense view of the world to discover the new truths, however absurd the necessary ideas seemed to be. They were not *absurd* ideas really, they were *necessary*, and only absurd to their everyday senses.

Dr Schmidt's experiments with the circle of lights and the electronic coin tosser show that a machine can be influenced by some people to a small but significant degree. However this is a very different matter from someone lightly stroking a teaspoon until it bends and the bowl drops off. By any stretch of the senses, an absurd claim.

So, in the next chapter, I want to look both at the claims of people who say that they *can* bend metal in this way, and at some experiments which are being done to investigate this most unlikely of events. This part of the paranormal is called 'psychokinesis' (sometimes 'telekinesis') and actually involves more interesting phenomena than just the bending of teaspoons.

7. Spoon Benders and Others

What do I see on the stills of Uri Geller stroking a spoon? I see him holding a teaspoon and stroking it; after a while, it bends and finally breaks in two. At least that is true if the frames of the film are in their actual sequence. As a matter of fact I do not find that film at all interesting, because it is not an experiment; the film was made some time ago, and all I can do now is to talk to the director or Uri Geller about what happened in the past. We cannot be sure where the spoon came from and we do not actually know whether Geller bent it with ordinary pressure from his hands. However, by looking at the actual film in motion, I can get a little more information because his fingers do not appear to be touching the spoon

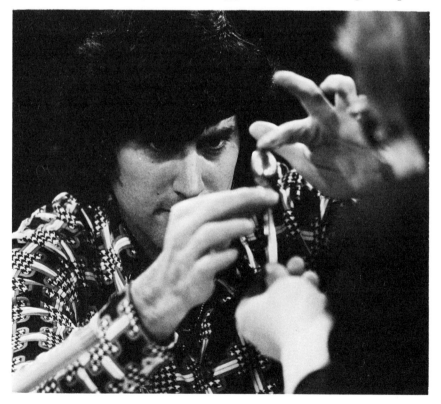

Fig. 36
Uri Geller bending a spoon, apparently by paranormal means. A still can never provide conclusive evidence, although a continuous film is harder to fake. (See Fig. 56.)

with any force, certainly not enough to bend it: but this is still not nearly sufficient information. An experimenter has to declare everything he did very clearly indeed, so that other people have a chance of repeating his work.

In the television series, I straightened a piece of wire by stroking it. Well, that is what it looked like! Actually, the wire is made of a special alloy which has a 'memory' of what shape it was in when it was first made. It is called Nitinol. If it was made *straight* and you then bend it by hand, when you heat it, it straightens up again. So when I stroked it in front of the camera what I really did was to move the wire into a stream of hot air and so it straightened. There was nothing paranormal about that. A thick teaspoon, however, is a different matter. Also in the programme, I bent a teaspoon made of perfectly hard metal. Now I could have bent it by hand pressure too. So I clipped the handle onto a letter balance, so that when I touched the spoon, you could see how much pressure I put on it with my finger. The spoon bent and finally the bowl dropped off. This time I used a spoon made from a special alloy which melts at about the temperature of boiling water. So, once again, when I started stroking it I actually moved it slightly into a stream of hot air, so the heat softened it, then bent it and finally melted it altogether. That is another bad experiment because I did not declare everything about the spoon metal.

One might conclude that there is nothing paranormal in metal bending, but that is not the case at all. It is an interesting phenomenon and quite central to the question of whether the mind can affect matter. By the pledges I have made to you so far, there ought to be some good experiments on metal bending. There are, and some of the results are very interesting. However, there is another problem we ought to look at at this stage.

Because the results of experiments like metal bending are *so* odd and *so* bizarre, the precautions experimenters have had to take are much more stringent than in any other area of research science. As I have suggested earlier, I sometimes think that if the standards of rigour which are used in some experiments on the paranormal were applied to experiments in ordinary science, half of the results there would fall apart. Why are such special precautions necessary?

Science is by its very nature extremely conservative, and this is thoroughly to the advantage of science. Any new concept or idea has to withstand the most rigorous and searching scrutiny before it is accepted. That this is often overdone is obvious; bad temper and polemic often creep in. On balance, however, it is better than allowing cant and superstition to rule reason.

So there is a tremendous reluctance to allow the stranger areas of the paranormal like psychokinesis any credence at all, because they upset a lot of preconceived notions. That is perfectly reasonable. Most of ordinary science works very well. It *is* repeatable, it *is* reliable and it *is* consistent. It is particular areas of science itself like the new physics which are now changing and suggesting a world view in which psychokinesis is possible.

For example, ordinary physics and biology would say that the energy binding the atoms of a teaspoon together is far too great for a soft watery organ like the brain to emit sufficient energy to alter the atoms enough to make the spoon bend. That by itself is true; there is no way I can see myself sending out enough energy from my brain to do it. Later on, however, I will be describing new ideas in physics which suggest that this is an over-simple way of looking at the connection between subject and teaspoon.

How can a brain do that? We would have to have some sort of power generator in our heads which could give off that sort of energy. So, if it happens, there must be some other explanation, and the real problem we have to face here is that some very experienced scientists are doing well controlled experimental work which suggests that it *does* happen.

This is what they did. First, they had to find a device which would measure metal bending. Of course, you will object that that is totally unnecessary: you just look and see metal bending for yourself. But that is only if the bending is big enough, which is called *macroscopic* bending; this long word is opposite to *microscopic*. Microscopic bending, according to the proper use of words, is bending which cannot be seen with the unaided eye. The experimenters in fact suspected that some cases of paranormal metal bending were probably *microscopic*, in that the metal would only show very, very small deflections, which the eye could not in fact see.

They therefore used a tiny sensor like the ones in Fig. 37 and attached it to one piece of metal with a special glue. The sensor is called a strain gauge and it can record very, very small movements in metal. Remember, a *sensor* is a device designed to give a *particular* signal when it detects a *particular* event. A thermometer is a *sensor*, because it gives a *signal* about *heat*. The signal is the level of the mercury in the tube. In a strain gauge the signals first go to an amplifier to make them bigger, and then on to a pen recorder to make the bigger signals visible. When the metal is deformed or bent very, very slightly, the strain gauge sends out a large signal about the bend through the apparatus, and the pen recorder makes a picture of it.

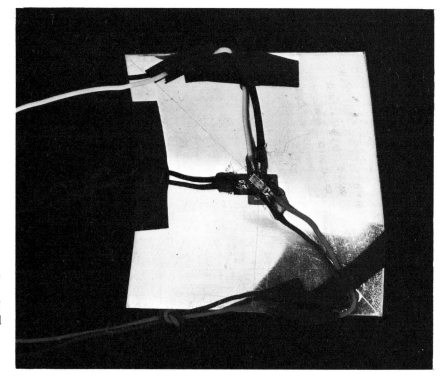

Fig. 37
A metal plate used in
experiment by
Professor Hasted.
Three strain gauges are
mounted, on top of
each other, at angles of
120°. Deflection should
therefore appear on all
three at once when
bending occurs.

Fig. 38
Diagrammatic view of
the record produced by
a strain gauge. A gauge
may produce a record
of bending too small to
be seen by the naked
eye, but larger than
deflections due to
noise.

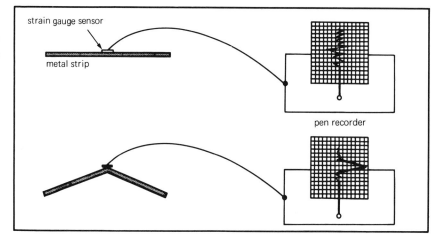

That looks far too sensitive. How can we be sure that the strain gauge would not produce a signal without any bending of the metal? Could it not just go off by itself? Yes, it could and does. So the first question we have to ask anyone using it is how they got over that particular difficulty. Any scientist using a new piece of equipment carries out what he calls a *calibration*. This means that he sets up the whole apparatus and just leaves it running by itself to see how much *noise* it produces. The word *noise* in this sense means only the force and number of spurious signals the machine produces by itself before it is set to work detecting signals. Once the *noise* level is recorded and measured, any larger signal the machine produces when it is detecting signals can be confidently assumed to be real and not spurious.

John Hasted is a large and friendly man with an acute, critical mind. He thinks for himself. He is Professor of Physics at Birkbeck College in the University of London and has for some years now been doing experiments on paranormal metal bending. There are as many different approaches to physics as there are physicists and John Hasted's is one of pure experimentation. If you talk to him about theory he will discuss matters with you courteously and with interest. But get him onto experiments, and his eyes light up and he starts to move quickly, sketch on the board and construct models of ideas with whatever is to hand.

In the basement of Birkbeck College, he has set up a laboratory to investigate people who say they can bend metal with their minds. First there is a screened room. This is a small cubicle made of aluminium sheet. It prevents spurious electrical signals getting in. Birkbeck College is full of physicists who are doing experiments which generate electrical and electronic signals, and these easily penetrate laboratory walls and interfere with other nearby equipment.

Inside the cubicle there is a chair where the subject sits. In front of the chair, the small strip of metal to be experimented on is suspended. Attached to the metal is the small strain gauge. A cable leads from the gauge to a bench outside the cubicle where the amplifier and the pen recorder are located. Between the piece of metal and the subject, there is a ring-shaped coil which will detect if the subject stretches forward actually to touch the metal.

We come now to the extraordinary feature of John Hasted's experiments. He now has a considerable body of evidence to show that some people can, without touch, cause the metal to bend enough to make the strain gauge register deflection many times larger than the top level of the noise in the apparatus. Could this sort of signal be generated spuriously from some other source?

Fig. 39
Professor Hasted in his
laboratory at Birkbeck
College, London.
Behind is the
metal-screened booth
in which subjects are
placed for
metal-bending
experiments.

[1] J. B. Hasted, *The
Metal-benders*,
Routledge and Kegan
Paul, London, 1981

To guard against this possibility, Professor Hasted has built a
'dummy' recording circuit alongside the real one, so that if any
spurious signal does get generated somewhere other than in the
metal, the 'dummy' circuit will record it as well. Finally, he
records electrical activity on the surface of the shielded cubicle as
well, to see whether any unwanted information is being generated
there. [1]

John Hasted has now completed many thousands of individual
experiments showing significant strain-gauge deflections with
young subjects. One problem he found with early experiments
was that the laboratory situation upset several of his subjects. To
solve this, he has also designed portable apparatus so that he can
visit the home of the subject. In this way, he takes the laboratory to
the subject rather than vice versa.

At the time of writing this section, I have just been to a meeting
of scientists where Professor Hasted gave an account of his latest
work. The question he set out to answer was this. If, he argued, the
metal was bent paranormally and the strain gauge showed a
significant deflection, then would there be any *internal* changes
in the metal which could be measured? To experiment on this he

Fig. 40
One of the problems of paranormal experimentation is that the tension of a laboratory situation may prevent the powers under investigation from appearing. One means Professor Hasted has devised to overcome this is the use of 'paperclip scrunching' as a test. Clips are inside a glass sphere – here of diameter 127 mm with an opening of 3 mm. The opening appears to be essential, but it is so small that attempts to reproduce the scrunching by normal means have never been wholly successful. As yet, the results must remain inconclusive.

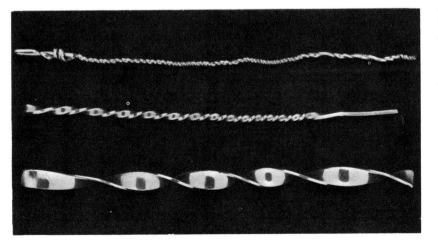

Fig. 41
More examples of the bending achieved by Professor Hasted's subjects. Of interest is that the twisting is so tight that to attempt it by mechanical means usually results in the metal shearing rather than twisting.

used a technique which sounds difficult, but in essence is very easy to understand. The method is called 'Rutherford Back Scattering' after Ernest Rutherford, one of the great pioneer scientists of early atomic research.

Fig. 42
A graph showing the results of one back-scattering experiment. The measurement is done by an independent laboratory, which would make it difficult to fake the results. The graph shows the number (N) of atoms of caesium per square centimetre at different depths in a sheet of aluminium. The depth is given in Angström degrees (Å), a measure of one hundred millionth of a metre.

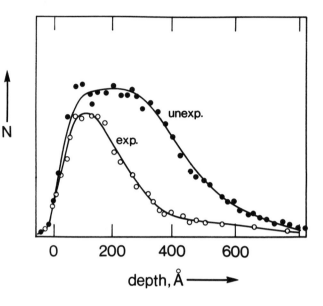

It is possible to 'inject' other atoms deep into a piece of metal so that they end up rather like peas in a jelly in various positions. Then by subjecting the piece of metal to a particular radiation, you can plot where the injected 'foreign' atoms are inside the metal. This technique was used to investigate a Frenchman who claimed to bend metal paranormally. [2] And John Hasted has now shown that there is a change in the position of the foreign injected atoms after the piece of metal had been exposed to a putative metal bender.

[2] C. M. Crussard and J. Bouvaist, *Memoires Scientifiques Révue Metallurgique*, Paris, February 1978

It is difficult to see how anyone could possibly cause internal changes like this in the metal, unless, of course, one is going to assume that there was some elaborate conspiracy involving subjects, John Hasted, laboratory technicians, metallurgists and so on.

I faced Stephen North, one of John Hasted's most successful young subjects, with the accusation that he was faking the whole thing. His reply was low key and sincere. Here is a transcript of how he replied:

KP: Stephen, you've been doing these experiments with Professor Hasted for a long time now and trying to bend metal by paranormal means. What does it feel like inside when you're doing the experiments?

SN: There's very little physical sensation, but it's certainly very important for me to be in a relaxed state of mind. It doesn't work very well when I try to concentrate.

KP: So when you're really trying to do it very hard it doesn't work?

SN: No, it doesn't; it's essential to be relaxed.

KP: Is it as if it catches you out, that it happens when you've turned your mind away from it?

SN: Yes, that's right.

KP: Do you feel very different from other people because you can do this?

SN: No, I'm – in fact I find, certainly amongst my generation and my friends, they all accept it and, you know, treat me normally. A few adults aren't very willing to treat me as a normal person...

KP: They treat you as some sort of freak, do they?

SN: Yes, but it doesn't make me feel any different. I lead a completely normal life.

KP: If an adult comes to you and says, look, I don't believe you're doing it, how do you feel about that?

SN: Well, if I was in their position, if I was in the audience watching a television programme about this or something similar, I would feel sceptical about it because I haven't actually seen it proved. But I know it happens and I know that I can do it and all I can hope is that gradually I'll be able to convince more people.

KP: Do you think it's something you could teach to other people? Is there some sort of form in your mind as to how it works, or is it too odd to talk about?

SN: Certainly I don't know how I can do it, but there are ways I can stop it from happening. For instance, when I first started to do it, everything in my house began to bend, all the cutlery bent and gradually I found I could stop that when I wanted to, and I can stop from damaging my watch or my own keys. But I don't think it can be taught, but I believe that everybody can probably do it; it's just finding how to.

KP: Do you think the ability to do it will stay with you or is it something you expect might disappear as you get older?

SN: Certainly I think it would disappear if I left it, if I allowed my mind to concentrate on other things.

KP: Do you want to hang on to it?

SN: Yes, I do.

KP: You would like to hang on to it?

SN: Yes, I would.

KP: What does it mean to you as a person?

SN: It's very important. I want to find out what it is and what's causing it.

KP: Have you any idea in your own mind as to what could be causing it?

SN: Not really. I believe that I'm simply focussing some kind of energy which science doesn't yet understand.

I then asked Professor Hasted how he came to start work on metal bending; it seems such a strange thing for a physicist to be doing, to look at something which is so bizarre. He replied:

Fig. 43
Spoons bent by
Professor Hasted's
subject Julie Knowles.

Well, physics itself is much more magical and bizarre than that. Down on the atomic scale I can't tell you the position of an atom exactly; I don't even know if an atom exists. It only probably exists. It could even be in two places at once. I don't know how many dimensions we're in; I don't know if our space is simple or complex. All of these things are far more bizarre than just a piece of metal deforming.

At first I was surprised by this reply, but now having had long conversations with several of the world's best physicists, I can only say that time and time again, the same sort of comment was made; that they were sure that the new physics was revealing a view of the universe which was indeterminate, inseparable into parts and utterly strange to our senses.

What is more difficult to grasp is that they were also finding that it was not possible to observe anything without assuming right at the start, that the *mind* is connected with the *matter* that the *mind* is observing.

So now, back to physics.

8. Realities that Failed

Supposing we now agree that a number of well designed experiments show that paranormal metal bending can occur; it still does not tell us how a soft watery organ like the brain can do what you would normally need a blow-torch to do. The problem seems to be that so far we have been looking at the brain as if it could send out some sort of energy beam which melts metal like a laser, and we agree the brain cannot do anything like that. So now we have to move on and try to understand what happens if that is not the answer. To do that I want to look at a part of the new physics which looks completely unreasonable to the commonsense mind: and that does not sound at all hopeful, because physics is *always* reasonable.

Remember that Einstein showed us that there was no single reality and that what we see depends on where and when we are. Now I want to look beyond Einstein at three tremendously important statements science made about the way the universe works and the way physicists see it. They all came to the fore about 1927, the year I was born, and they took physics onwards to a point where the paranormal bending of metal was no longer an absolute impossibility. The three statements go like this.

First: The world revealed by experiments in physics *cannot* be understood by the senses alone.

Second: Physics has absolutely abandoned any attempt at describing reality and says instead that physics only reveals *connections* and *interactions* between our minds and the world outside us.

Third: The act of observing something alters the something you have been trying to observe.

In Fig. 44 a bulb is giving out two beams of light. One is hitting a prism and the other is hitting a metal plate. The plate is electrically charged, as you can see on the meter. If an electrical voltage is applied to a metal plate, the surface of the plate becomes *charged* in exactly the same way as you can *charge* the surface of a plastic pen by rubbing it on cloth. You can visualise the charge as

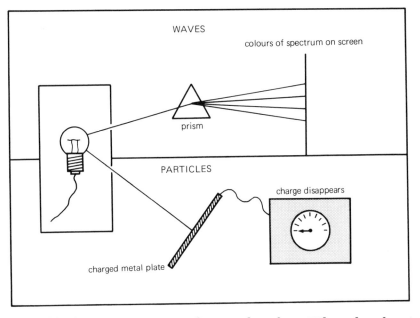

WAVES

colours of spectrum on screen

prism

PARTICLES

charge disappears

charged metal plate

Fig. 44
A summary of the
evidence for the dual
nature of light. When
light is passed through
a prism, it breaks up
into colours. The best
explanation for this is
that light is made of
waves. When light
from the *same* source
is directed at an
electrically charged
plate, the charge
disappears. The best
explanation for this is
that light is particles.
But light from the
same source cannot be
both particles and
waves at the same
time. This is the
paradox of
complementarity. It
was resolved by Niels
Bohr, who suggested
that the results you get
from an experiment
depend on the
experiment. He
proposed that we
cannot study the
properties of light, but
only our interactions
with it. This view of
things inevitably
connects observer and
reality.

a row of little + or − signs on the metal surface. When the plate is discharged, by earthing it, the signs leak away.

If the beam of light goes through the prism it breaks up into colours and the best way of explaining the colours is to say that light from the bulb is made of waves, which are of many different wavelengths and the different wavelengths have different colours. When another light beam *from the same bulb* hits the metal plate, the electric charge on the plate starts to dwindle and go away, and the best way of explaining that is to say that the beam of light is a stream of particles like small cannon balls which blasted the electric charges clean out of the surface of the piece of metal. Obviously you cannot have the same beam of light being both waves and particles.

Supposing we now do the experiment again and this time make quite sure that we have synchronised the two halves of the experiment. We can be sure that one beam strikes the prism at exactly the same time that the other beam strikes the metal plate and the same results will be achieved.

Now we have an absolutely massive problem. We are forced to conclude that light *can* be both particles and waves. What is worse, light from the *same* source of light can be both waves and particles at the *same* time. That was exactly the problem the physicists faced. Because what their experiments told them very, very clearly was just that: a beam of light could be both particles and waves − or it could have both the *properties* of particles and waves, which is an obvious and complete paradox.

The physicists discovered an even more disturbing aspect of this paradox: the properties of waves and the properties of very small particles are just not compatible; they cannot exist together. So now their dilemma was like this: the same light can be both waves and particles at the same time and the properties of waves and particles are mutually exclusive.

It would take an unusually original mind to solve a paradox like that. The man who did solve it was certainly unusual. He was Danish, a physicist and a Nobel Prize winner, Niels Bohr. His solution was perhaps one of the greatest steps in the foundations of physics, and for the first time connected mind and matter together in a fundamentally logical way. Looking now at what he said, it seems deceptively simple, but the effect on physics was shattering.

His solution to the paradox was to say that the experiment was not measuring the properties of light, but measuring the *interaction* of light with the experiment and so with the experimenter. This simple statement destroyed for ever the idea that there was an objective, real world out there and said instead that there was a real functional and indivisible connection between observer, experiment and object.

If you design an experiment to discover the wave-like properties of light you will discover the wave-light properties of light and if you design an experiment to discover the particle-like properties of light you will discover light particles. Which is very much like saying we can shape an object with our mind by designing a particular sort of experiment with our mind.

Otto Frisch, one of the discoverers of nuclear fission, put it like this:

We should not ask what light really is. Particles and waves are both aspects of the human mind, designed to help us speak about the behaviour of light in different circumstances. With Bohr we gave up the main concept of reality, the idea that the world is made up of things, waiting for us to discover their nature. The world is made up by us, out of our experiences and the concepts we create to link them together. [1] [My emphasis.]

[1] O. Frisch, *The Nature of Matter*, Thames and Hudson, London, 1972

This solution to the paradox by Niels Bohr is known as 'complementarity': this deceptively simple and beautifully elegant idea will recur again and again in this book. The wave and the particle results are complementary to each other, but they are abstractions, not reality. The solution had profound implications. The physicists no longer believed that they were studying the properties of light, but only their *interactions* with light. They interacted with light in a particular way by designing a particular experiment.

The experiment became their means of establishing a *connection* with light by *interacting* with it. Things like elementary, very small particles vanished. Niels Bohr wrote: 'Isolated material particles are abstractions, their properties being definable and observable only through their *interaction* with the other system.' [2] [My italics.]

The concept of the elementary particle, a small, cannon-ball-like component of matter is another abstraction. Many of the properties of one elementary particle, the electron, for example, can be visualised as if the electron really is a small bullet; it has properties of speed, momentum and mass. However, other, equally valid, properties reveal it as a cloud of probability holding an electric charge. These are both complementary views. There are now nearly one hundred elementary particles each with different properties and each with some aspects of a small bullet and each with other complementary properties.

In the same book, Bohr also wrote: 'Independent reality in the ordinary physical sense can be ascribed neither to the phenomena nor to the agencies of observation.'

Looking at the general implications of complementarity, what it means in our search for a rational basis to the paranormal is that observer, instruments and experimental object are inextricably linked in a triad. Mind, machinery and matter are an indivisible

[2] N. Bohr, *Atomic Physics and the Description of Nature*, Cambridge University Press, 1934

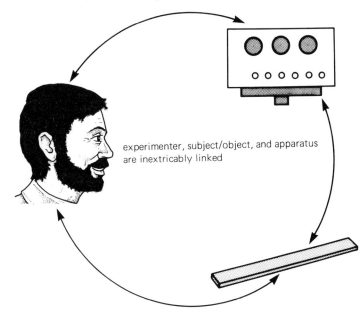

experimenter, subject/object, and apparatus are inextricably linked

Fig. 45
In all experiments, there is an unbreakable connection between the observer, the subject, and the object being measured by the instruments.

whole in which we are forced by virtue of logic and reason to work. Gone for ever was the Newtonian illusion that we could study nature as separated, isolated observers. This Newtonian standpoint is often called 'dualism'. A 'dualist' believes in independence of mind from matter whereas a 'monist' holds that there is only one undivided whole in which our minds are embedded inextricably. Complementarity meant starkly and simply that mind can *never* be separated from matter when we are trying to understand matter.

To understand how physicists now look at matter, I would like you to imagine that I have suddenly developed academic delusions of grandeur and have appointed myself Professor of Table Investigation.

I begin my experiments by rapping my knuckle against a wooden table and I am reassured by the noise of the rap and the feeling in my knuckle. Both sensations tell me without question that the wood is hard and the table is really there. I can also verify the hard outline of the table with my eyes, and this fits the 'knuckle experience' exactly. I do the same thing with the same table the next day and the next day and everything remains consistent. The table is a real table, and I will not have anybody monkeying with the idea that the table is anything except an ordinary table which I can rap.

I now decide that the table is interesting and want to know what it is made of. Experience tells me that wood comes from trees, and books will tell me what the microscopic structure of wood looks like. Just to verify this, I cut a small shaving from the table, cut very thin slices from the shaving, stain them, mount them on a glass slide, and look at them down a light microscope. I am totally reassured. Before me are the beautiful arcades and tunnels of the wood cells. Everything fits the text book.

I then cut even thinner slices of wood and put them in an electron microscope, which lets me examine the wood at a magnification of two million times. Again I am reassured. A whole landscape of new structural detail emerges and I can even see the dim, smudged outlines of individual large molecules in one cell wall. Once again my confidence remains unshaken, because I can compare all these results with those of other professors of table investigation. At the next international conference of table investigators we can all relax over a drink in the evening and congratulate ourselves expensively on the consistency of our results, and on how well we really do understand what a table is and how nobody else should argue with us.

Back in the laboratory, however, I am subject to some niggling doubts and look vainly around for an even more powerful micro-scope. But there is no such thing, so I have to go to a chemist and ask him what wood is made of. He tells me that it is mainly cellulose, and that the molecular smudges I have been looking at are real images and groups of real cellulose molecules, and that these molecules are made up of carbon and hydrogen atoms. Still reassured about my belief in the church of reason, I decide that since the table is made of carbon and hydrogen I had better look into the structure of carbon and hydrogen atoms. So I begin to study atomic theory.

Now the trouble really begins, and my vision of a Nobel Prize for contributions to the science of table investigation disappears. I cannot rap carbon and hydrogen atoms with my knuckles, and I cannot see carbon and hydrogen atoms.

There is much worse in store. I now find that the carbon and hydrogen atoms are made of what I am told are 'elementary particles', and that these have names which distinguish each one from another and cannot under any circumstances be seen.

Each atom has a nucleus and the nucleus is made up of particles called nucleons. There are two varieties of nucleon: the proton and the neutron. I then find that there are other particles called electrons which are circling the nucleus at very high speeds. I also find that these particles have qualities of mass, spin, electric charge and resonance. *Resonance* on the atomic scale is the same as on the large scale: a bell hanging next to another bell hit with a hammer will ring in *resonance*. Not only can I not rap nucleons or electrons, I cannot see them, touch them or feel them; and I cannot weigh them or spin them or get a shock from them. I am also asked to accept that the atom in which these very high-speed move-ments are taking place is nearly all empty space.

I look again at the table. Not only is no part of it in visible motion, it does not give me an electric shock, it is not spinning and it does not resonate. No edge or surface is frothing or seething in motion and no part of it, except for the worm holes, is empty space.

I go back to the particle physicists, tell them they are liars and demand to be shown an electron or nucleon. I receive the answer that electrons and nucleons cannot be put into bottles and they only have a *tendency* to exist. Physicists here talk about a probability cloud, a phrase which describes the strange situation where, although the particles do have properties which enable differences between them to be measured, no one can say whether such a particle is at a particular location in space at a particular time.

In one leap I have left the world of the hard and tangible and entered a new world where there are no hard edges, but only moving miasmata of change and chance. Nothing is certain any more and nothing can be seen or manipulated by the unaided human eye or hand. The table has disappeared in a cloud of uncertainty. However, I can still rap the table; or go quietly mad.

This description of table investigation is taken from my book, *The Quest for Gaia*. [3]

[3] K. Pedler, *The Quest for Gaia*, Souvenir Press, London, 1979; Granada, London, 1981

So where have we got to? The physicist's current view of nature is that mind is connected with matter; matter is composed largely of space with constant movements and change occurring in that space. The space itself is linked with time, and observations only reveal interactions and connections and not properties.

The whole fabric of the universe becomes much less hard-edged and certain and can best be understood in these terms. I must emphasise that these views of nature have not emerged from some creative wilfulness on the part of the physicists but because they explain more unknowns and enable us to understand more phenomena (and remember, by phenomena, I mean that of which the senses or the mind are aware).

Most of the work was based also on fiendishly difficult mathematics and not on supposition alone. Even mathematics had come under scrutiny. Bertrand Russell wrote: 'Mathematics may be defined as the subject in which we never know what we are talking about, nor whether what we are saying is true.' [4] Typically, this is not a dismissal of mathematics but a carefully worded doubt. 'Know' and 'true' are the key words in this passage.

[4] Quoted in W. Heisenberg, *Across the Frontiers*, Harper and Row, New York, 1974

The final blow to an objective and hard-edged reality was struck by another physicist of the time: Werner Heisenberg. He was looking at the behaviour of elementary particles and discovered the awesome truth that if he made *one* measurement on a particle, he couldn't make another, *accurate* one, simultaneously. One measurement blurred the other. What he discovered was called the Uncertainty Principle and was gradually extended to the statement that: You cannot observe a thing without altering the thing by observing it.

Supposing I want to measure the pressure inside a car tyre. To do so, I have to let some air out of the tyre into the gauge to get a reading on the dial. If I let air out of the tyre, the pressure inside the tyre is lower than it was before I attached the gauge. So the measurement of the pressure with the gauge has *altered* the pressure inside the tyre. By *measuring* the pressure, I have *altered* the pressure. So there is no such thing as an accurately objective measurement. [5]

[5] After O. Frisch, *The Nature of Matter*, Thames and Hudson, London, 1972

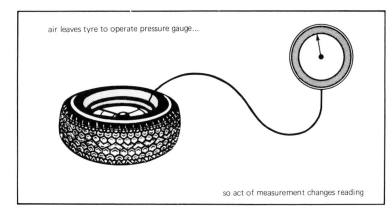
air leaves tyre to operate pressure gauge...

so act of measurement changes reading

Fig. 46
An example of the
Uncertainty Principle
as applied generally.
When the air pressure
in a car tyre is
measured, some air is
let out of the tyre into
the gauge – so the
gauge records a
slightly lower
pressure. The act of
measurement changes
the quantity being
measured.

I must point out that the Uncertainty Principle was a precisely formulated mathematical idea about elementary particles. Heisenberg actually showed that it was impossible to measure both the position and momentum of a particle simultaneously. The measurement of one actively blurred measurement of the other and vice versa. The principle has been hotly debated by physicists ever since, and they still play the game of 'Beat the Uncertainty Principle'. It caused Niels Bohr to say that the new physics forces 'the necessity of a final renunciation of the classical ideal of causality and a radical revision of our attitude towards the problem of physical reality'. [6]

It is interesting to look at Niels Bohr's coat-of-arms which he designed. In the centre is the Chinese symbol of yin-yang unity. A picture of it can be found in a memorial book to him. [7]

So how can we relate all that to bending metal with the mind? What it all adds up to is this: physics no longer even pretends to study a real hard-edged world, but only the interaction of the *mind* of the physicist *with* the world. The two seem to become absolutely indivisible, and some of the scientists who created the new physics knew this very clearly:

'Subject and object are only one. The barrier between them cannot be said to have broken down as a result of recent experience in the physical world, for this barrier *does not exist.*' (Erwin Schrödinger)

'The common division of the world into subject and object, inner world and outer world, body and soul is no longer adequate . . .' (Werner Heisenberg)

'The world of physics is a world of shadows, we were not aware of it; we thought we were dealing with the *real* world.' (Erwin Schrödinger)

[6] N. Bohr, *Atomic Theory and Human Knowledge*, John Wiley, New York, 1958

[7] S. Rozenthal (ed.), *Niels Bohr*, North Holland Publishing, Amsterdam, 1967

Fig. 47
Sir Arthur Eddington,
astronomer, Fellow of
the Royal Society
(1882–1944): 'The stuff
of the world is
mind-stuff.'

Others took this even further:

'The stuff of the universe is mind-stuff.' (Sir Arthur Eddington)

'The universe looks less and less like a great machine and more and more like a great thought.' (Sir James Jeans)

So if physics holds that there is no absolutely real outside world but only an interaction between our conscious minds and the world, then the idea of metal bending is no longer impossible. We no longer have to visualise a hypothetical laser beam lancing out from the mind to the metal, but only an *interaction* between the mind and the metal in a *particular reality*.

Now I want to make something absolutely clear. The new physics does not *explain* the paranormal. What it does do, however, is to provide a framework of ideas in which it is more acceptable. There are in fact experiments now being done in physics which *are* beginning to show that there may be more of an explanation and I will be having a look at those in the last chapter. These are in their early stages and the debate about them is active indeed.

Now that we have had a good look at matter and the enormous changes which have taken place in the physicists' view of nature, the other ingredient in our mix is the mind. The word itself carries little meaning as a concept, but we all agree that our *experience* is that we have an 'I' that we think with.

9. The 'I' That I Think With

To discover the connections and interactions between 'mind' and 'matter', some sort of definition of mind ought to be possible. It ought to be possible also to extend the definition to include what is meant by the 'conscious mind' and by 'consciousness' as well.

If we have already agreed that you and I can reach some understanding about these words by comparing experience, this is a beginning. We can agree that we recognise consciousness by experience. Consciousness is an experiencing state in which we are aware of information from the senses, we are aware of the outside world and we are aware that we can think, imagine and take action.

From this we can also recognise unconsciousness as an absence of these combined awarenesses. The difference here being that we can recognise unconsciousness, but not whilst we are unconscious. We need to be conscious to be aware of a previous state of unconsciousness. If we then analyse these statements a little further, we can also probably agree that all these experiences are due to a thinking, experiencing 'I', and that this 'I', the knowledge of self, is the nearest approach we can make to any agreed definition of mind, at least at this stage.

To attempt anything more elaborate brings us straight up against the Uncertainty Principle of Heisenberg: that we cannot observe anything without altering that something by the act of observation. This principle has often been restated. Professor Andrade wrote: 'Observation means interference with what we are observing.' [1]

According to Kenneth Wilber, 'Objective measurement and verification could no longer be the mark of absolute reality, because the measured object could never be separated from the measuring subject, the measured and the measurer. The verified and the verifier, at this level, are one and the same.' [2]

This blurring between subject and object is one of the cornerstones of the new physics and centrally important to any general understanding of the paranormal, since it means very clearly

[1] E. N. da C. Andrade, *An Approach to Modern Physics*, Doubleday, New York, 1957

[2] K. Wilber, *The Spectrum of Consciousness*, Quest Books, Theosophical Publishing House, Wheaton, Illinois; London; 1977

indeed that there will always be connections and interactions between things and events we study and one of those connections will be the mind.

The principle of complementarity *demands* a connection between mind, experiment and subject and in the same way when we try and set a clearer idea of mind and consciousness, the same difficulty arises, which is made more severe because the mind cannot study itself, since the act of self-study will alter the mind.

There is a way round this dilemma. Start lower down the scale in an approach to the mind and then to see what happens when the mind (that is, the something that we agree by experience that we have) is changed. When a scientist wants to study something he cannot understand, he changes it in a deliberate and measured way, hoping that the changes will reveal some aspects of it.

We can all agree we have a brain inside our skulls. We can also agree that we look out from the inside of our heads at the outside world with our consciousness. That is another way of saying by experience: we have a mind. So is it possible to discover the location of something we can only experience? One logical philosopher, A. J. Ayer, refused to study the mind at all because, he said, 'it has no locus' which is Latin for saying he did not know where it is.

Supposing I was to turn into a Dr Frankenstein and lop someone's head off and stick it on some tubes to keep it alive, the someone would still look out at the world from the head as a conscious human being, although he might be a little upset. So in a general way, what we can talk about as the mind appears to have some sort of a *place* in the brain, and the brain gives out electrical signals which change according to what sort of state you are in. For example, when you are asleep, particular waves appear and when you wake up they almost disappear.

These electrical recordings from the scalp, called electro-encephalograms (e.e.g's.), however, are only general manifestations of a tumult of information exchange going on between the millions of nerve cells that make up the physical brain.

Someone once said that the e.e.g. is like putting a microphone on the roof of King's Cross railway station hoping to pick up the sound of a single train.

One view of the brain is that it is two brains in one: the left brain and the right brain. There is quite good evidence that the left brain is concerned with logical, mechanical tasks and the right brain is more concerned with intuition and creativity. Although there are massive connections between the two, they do seem to be related to these different sorts of behaviour.

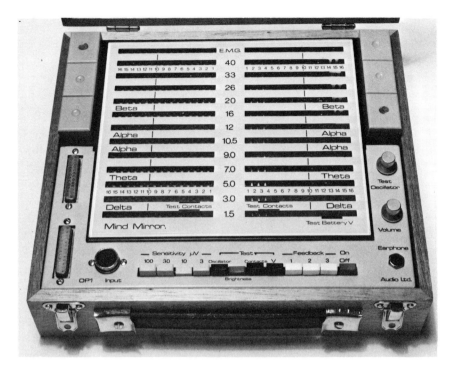

Fig. 48
The 'Mind Mirror' is a modified electro-encephalograph which displays the balance of activity between the left and right sides of the brain.

The machine shown here is a modified e.e.g. apparatus, and is so arranged as to show the electrical activities of the 'left' brain as a line of lights on the left and the activities of the 'right' brain as a line of lights on the right. It is called the 'Mind Mirror' and I have used it myself.

During the experiment, some Bach was playing on a 'hi-fi', and I found I could 'move' the lights from the left bank to the right bank by thinking about the calm, emotional perfection of the music and then to the left again by thinking about the logical, computer-like aspect of the same music. A sort of complementarity of music. I did not look at the lights while I was doing the experiment, because it was necessary to get into a quiet, reflective state to make it work.

I am not suggesting that these tiny voltages on the e.e.g. and the Mind Mirror coming from the brain are enough to bend metal. What the machines do tell me is that by *conscious* will I can change the *external* electrical records of my brain. If you allow also that there is an absolutely unbreakable connection between mind, experiment and object, and if you agree, too, that space and time are peculiar to where you are, then perhaps you can see that if metal bending turns out to be generally accepted as real, it is something that happens only between subject and experiment. It is almost as if they are bound together in a private universe while it happens, like the Mind Mirror and my brain. In fact, nearly everyone who can do these things, and also some of the experimenters, refer to a particular moment when a paranormal event occurs as being a time when their whole view of the world and their connection with it changes altogether.

One of the best known and most successful of subjects was Mrs Eileen Garrett, an American business woman with a long and extraordinary documented record of paranormal ability. For example, Arthur Young, the engineer inventor of the Bell helicopter, recalls a strange event with her:

...we'd had a severe helicopter accident in which the pilot and assistant were both killed. I felt very badly about it. I thought the machine had been at fault.... It was very curious, this sense of tremendous responsibility.... I took a piece of the helicopter blade to Eileen Garrett. She held it in her hand and said that the machine was all right but that the pilot had been on the verge of a nervous breakdown and was about to enter a monastery when the crash occurred.

I did not want to go back and ask the bereaved parents these questions and so I just forgot the whole thing. However, about a year later I went to see the man ... who had hired the pilot. He volunteered that 'that pilot was having a nervous breakdown and was about to enter a monastery'. This was a year after Eileen Garrett had told me the same thing. [3]

[3] Quoted in J. Mishlove, *The Roots of Consciousness*, Random House, New York, 1975

This is an anecdote, but the correlations are very impressive.

Dr Lawrence Le Shan spent a long time questioning people with paranormal ability like Eileen Garrett. He reports:

'When I approached them with this question [what is going on when it is done], they all said something similar. "Oh yes," they said, "when we are getting the paranormal information, the world looks quite different than at other times."' [4]

[4] L. Le Shan, *The Medium, the Mystic and the Physicist*, Turnstone Books, London, 1974

Eileen Garrett wrote: 'The supersensory experiences of clairvoyance trance, telepathy and so on, depend on a fundamental shift of one's awareness. The field of stimulation is itself changed.' [5]

So far I have been looking at the ability of the thinking 'I' to do something with an electrical record of the brain doing the thinking. By an act of will, we can change the electrical activity of the brain. Can we, however, make a useful connection between this action and the sensitive subject who can produce paranormal information, again by an act of will which causes them to shift into a different relationship?

[5] E. Garrett, *Awareness*, Creative Age Press, New York, 1943

'Ruth' is an American girl who lived a normal life until the age of fifteen when, on one awful night, an apparition of her father appeared beside her bed. The apparition terrified her because her father had raped her at the age of ten. After this first appearance, her life began to break up because the apparition occurred more and more frequently and with greater and greater reality. Ruth was not only able to see the apparition; she was able, too, to feel its touch, talk to it, smell it and be aware of its smell after it had gone.

American psychiatrist Dr Morton Schatzman has written a truly remarkable record of his time with her as therapist. [6] My point is *not* to discuss whether Ruth's apparition was 'really' there outside her head or not, but to describe an experiment Dr Schatzman did with her.

[6] M. Schatzman, *The Story of Ruth*, Duckworth, London, 1980

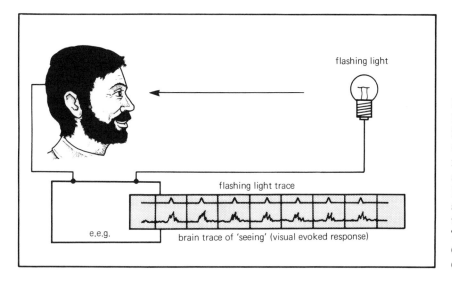

Fig. 49
If a light is regularly flashed in front of the eyes, an electrical recording from the seeing part of the brain (e.e.g.) will show signals corresponding to the flashing light. These signals are called the visual evoked response.

If electrodes similar to those used in e.e.g. work are fixed to the scalp on the back of the head, electrical signals can be recorded from the part of the brain that is concerned with seeing. Once again, however, the brain gives out a large quantity of signals which are not concerned with seeing and so, when a scientist wants to sort out the visual from the non-visual activity of the brain, he has to use a computer-driven averaging procedure.

Once the visual signals are separable from the 'noise', then if a light is regularly flashed at the eyes of the subject, the visual signals should be greater at the time of the flash. This is so, and it is called the 'visual evoked response', because it is an electrical response evoked by the visual process.

Ruth's visual evoked response was tested and found to be normal. Then it was tested again while she was experiencing a hallucination and it fell to about half its normal value. Ruth was tested again, this time using a chequerboard pattern as a visual stimulus. Her response was again normal. She was tested again while she was experiencing an apparition and the evoked response disappeared altogether.

After exhaustive tests, the doctors concluded that Ruth's brain was entirely normal, but that the ability to shut off the responses of her 'seeing' brain during experience of the apparition was entirely validated. Ruth could generate the apparitions to order: here is objective, outside evidence of a person who can will a very complex electrical activity of the brain to diminish or disappear.

So what does this tell us? It tells us that there is *external* objective evidence to be found of very complex and mind-like *internal* activity. To pursue this in a little more detail I now want to look at the work of a Canadian neurosurgeon Dr Wilder Penfield.

Ruth had an ability to suppress external, electrical activities of the brain by complex, internal mind-like processes. The 'I' *inside* her was producing responses *outside* her. Dr Penfield did the reverse, he electrically stimulated the surface of the conscious human brain exposed during neurosurgery. He used something *outside* the brain to produce effects which were *inside* the mind.

How can the patient be conscious with a hole in his head like that? Surely he would be in agony? Curiously enough, the brain itself does not feel pain and so the surgeon only has to give a local anaesthetic to the scalp and the skull. Once inside the whole procedure is painless.

Dr Penfield discovered something which helps us in our search for the mind. When he touched various parts of the brain with needles, giving a very small electric shock, you might expect that he would have evoked a simple body response like the twitch of an arm or pins and needles in the leg. Instead, what he found was that in some brain areas he produced an *intact whole memory*. A patient would say that a touch with the electric needle in one place evoked an entire thought – for example, 'I can see my bedroom window in the home I used to live in', or, 'I can smell hot doughnuts'.

That is what we, as owners of a *brain*, would experience as the *mind* at work. We might imagine a robot having its electronic brain stimulated to produce a twitch or a movement, but not to produce an intact human thought. Therefore we cannot conclude that the mind is the brain, but that they are very closely associated. If this seems to be a glimpse from the obvious, it does need discussion to avoid hasty conclusions.

One recent idea for which there is growing evidence is that the mind may exist inside the brain rather like a hologram. A hologram is a way of recording visual images photographically. It is

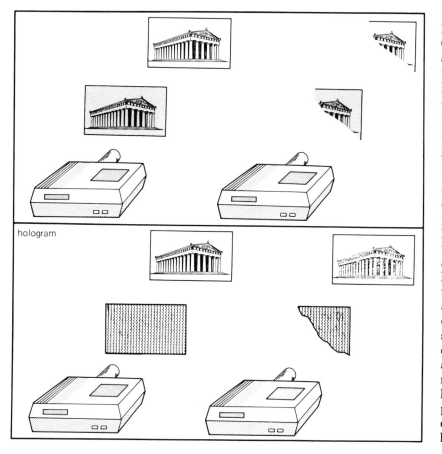

hologram

Fig. 50
One recent theory about the mind is that it is similar to a hologram. If an ordinary slide is projected, the whole picture appears on the screen. If the slide is broken and a piece projected, only the part of the picture corresponding to that piece appears. If a hologram is projected, the whole picture appears; if part of a hologram is projected, the whole picture still appears, but in less detail. In an ordinary slide, a piece corresponds exactly to a piece of the re-created picture. In a hologram, the entire picture is present in each part of the hologram.

produced with laser light and does not produce a negative picture of the subject on film, but a pattern of waves which is generated by mixing laser light which has not struck the object with laser light which has.

If I make an ordinary photographic negative of a chess piece and project it, I see a whole chess piece on the screen. If I smash the negative and put a bit of it back in the projector, I only see a bit of the chess piece corresponding to the bit of negative. One bit of the picture on each bit of the negative; a *part* in a *part*.

If I take a hologram of the same chess piece, the wave patterns of light bouncing off the chess piece are recorded on the negative and when it is specially projected, the wave patterns are reassembled into the picture. If I smash the hologram of the chess piece, I can still see the *whole* of the chess piece in *every part* of the plate, although the image will be fuzzier and show less detail. I repeat: the *whole* is in each *part*.

It used to be thought that the brain was composed of specific isolated centres: one for speech, one for movement, another for sensation and so on. Of course this still remains true at a large-scale level; that if one of those centres is removed, the function represented in that area is lost. Nevertheless, this is not universally true and for some of the more complex and mind-like activities, the hologram-mind idea proposes that the *whole* of the mind may be in every *part* of the brain, just as the *whole* of the image of the chess piece is in every *part* of the hologram. So how does that help us to understand the effect of mind on matter?

Because it creates the possibility that the mind may be much less fixed in the brain. That although it is somewhere inside the brain, it is a more mobile entity, not necessarily confined to a set of anatomical centres.

The debate as to exactly what and where the mind is, will continue unabated because it is absolutely central to understanding what we are as human beings. The work I have been describing suggests that a *connection* or *interaction* can be established between what we *experience* as mind and what an external experimenter will *measure* as on outside physical phenomenon. This is perhaps the best that can be achieved, since physics itself is saying very much the same thing; that there is no outside objective reality, and all we can do as observers is to study the connections and interactions between ourselves and nature by designing particular experiments.

The principle of complementarity in physics states also that the type of *experiment* we design specifies the type of *result* we get. Experiments designed to discover the wave aspects of light reveal the wave aspects of light and experiments designed to discover the particle aspects of light reveal the particle-like aspects of light. Wave ideas and particle ideas are both descriptions of an interaction between ourselves and light and are *not* inherent properties of light.

In exactly the same way, we can do experiments on the mind and discover that there are electrical phenomena associated with mind-like activity. Or we could take blood samples during experiments on mind-like activity and discover changes in the chemistry of the blood. In the first case we might conclude that the mind is driven electrically and in the second, conclude that the mind was run by chemicals. In neither case as observers would we have discovered anything about the *properties* of the mind; what we would have achieved is to describe aspects of our *interaction* and *connection* with the mind as observers.

The view of nature now proposed by physics is a much more mobile, flowing whole. The fixed mechanistic world of Newton has given way to a view that is more broadly based, but just as logical and rational. It is a view which only talks about flowing interactions and connections and not about rigidly locked structures in a fixed and motionless space and time.

Biology is certainly lagging behind physics in looking at living material, and when it catches up it may too reveal the body we live in and the mind we experience to be composed of more mobile and flowing events and structures. We too are made of atoms, protons, electrons and so we cannot escape the conclusion that our basic structure is similar in every way to the interconnected dynamic web of the non-living world. Allan Watts put it with delightful insight and wit:

A living body is not a fixed thing but a flowing event like a flame or a whirlpool. The shape alone is stable, for the substance is a stream of energy going in one end and out the other.

We are particular and identifiable wiggles on a stream that enters us in the form of light, heat, air, water, milk, bread, fruit, Beef Stroganoff, caviar and pâté de foie gras.

It goes out again as gas and excrement, and also as semen, babies, talk, politics, commerce, war, poetry and music. And philosophy. [7]

[7] A. Watts, *Does it Matter*, Vintage Books (Random House), New York, 1971

As I write this, an extraordinary account has been published[8] of a student at Sheffield University with an IQ of 126 and an honours degree in mathematics. The extraordinary part of the account is that the student has practically no cerebral cortex (what we have always assumed is the 'thinking' part of the brain), as measured by a brain scan. This again casts serious doubt on the relationship between the physical brain and the mind. By all traditional reasoning, this student would be more likely to be mentally subnormal with such a small amount of brain cortex. Perhaps because of his lack of the cortical material, his mind shifted into some other part of his brain rather like the hologram.

[8] *The Times*, London, 30 December 1980

I now want to deal with one of the strangest and most challenging areas of the paranormal. If the mind is more like the shifting wave patterns of a hologram, and perhaps mobile in the substance of the brain – could it leave the brain altogether and go somewhere else?

10. Minds on a Journey

'Out-of-body-experiences' have been described throughout history, and some people believe they may have given rise to the idea of the soul. The experience is often reported by people undergoing light anaesthesia and they describe the very clear and absolutely real (to them) experience of floating out of their body and being able to look down at themselves from a particular position in space. This position is more often than not above and to the left of the left shoulder. Sometimes people who are near death also have these experiences; there are several accounts by people who have been reported clinically dead. The experience is also sometimes associated with shock, following an accident, or during a severe illness.

An example quoted by Celia Green is fairly typical: 'I was sitting at the rear of a bus looking out through the window when without warning I found myself looking at myself from the stairs of the bus. All my senses, sight feelings and so on, seemed to be on the stairs; only my actual body remained on the seat.' [1]

[1] C. Green, *Out-of-body Experiences*, Hamish Hamilton, London, 1968

However, this is still an account of an *experience*. It is what someone is telling *us*; we cannot just accept it because a lot of people experience it. It would simply be anecdote or story telling and so, in the terms of this book, is inadmissible. We cannot dismiss anecdotes altogether; there is no reason why they should be more true or untrue than any other account, but here, once again, we come up against the absolutely fundamental distinction common both to the new physics and to the study of the paranormal: what is *inside* the mind of the person and what can be registered as an objective measurement *outside*. Since we cannot be certain that the mind has material substance, how then could we possibly look for evidence of the mind leaving the brain? The second part of the problem is that if there is an indissoluble connection between observer, experiment and the subject of the experiment, is the idea of trying to observe the mind in flight inevitably doomed to failure?

Dr Charles Tart is an experimental psychologist with a long

experience of experiments on the paranormal. He has written one of the most lucid books on the subject [2] and in conversation with him during the making of the series, I rapidly discovered that he had been over all the usual experimental pitfalls and discovered a few more for himself. He is an outgoing, generous personality but retains a wry critical base to his discussion. He experimented with someone whom he calls, for reasons of her privacy, 'Miss Z'.

Miss Z experienced many out-of-body experiences as a child, each lasting about a minute. They were so regular that in the end she became bored with them. Charles Tart knew Miss Z and began experiments with her using a sleep laboratory (psycho-physiological laboratory). A sleep laboratory or psycho-physiological laboratory is specially equipped to monitor and record all the usual body responses, like heart-rate, blood pressure, respiration rate and brain waves. The laboratory also has a comfortable quiet bedroom, where body and brain reaction can be studied while a subject sleeps through the night. Charles Tart wired Miss Z to various electronic recorders to monitor her brain waves, eye movements, skin resistance, blood pressure and pulse rate. This was to get a general idea of Miss Z's bodily and mental reactions while she was asleep.

Dr Tart then hid a five-digit, randomly selected number on a shelf above the couch where Miss Z was to try and have an 'out-of-body experience'. He then asked her to identify the number on the shelf while she was 'out of body'.

[2] C. Tart, *Psi*, E. P. Dutton, New York, 1977

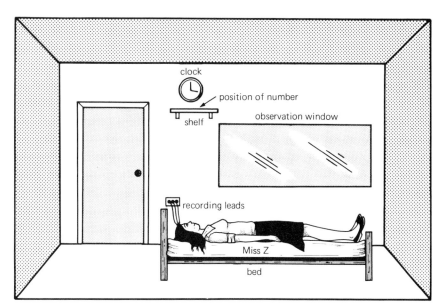

Fig. 51
Miss Z was placed in a sleep laboratory connected to an electro-encephalogram and other physiological monitors outside. The target number was placed on a shelf over her head. The recording leads from her scalp were too short for her to read the number by standing up to look, and had she removed the leads, the recording would have shown that.

On the first night, nothing happened. On the second night, she had an out-of-body experience. The time was 3.15 a.m. and at that time, her brain waves showed a highly unusual pattern; but there were no rapid eye movements which normally accompany dreams. She failed to identify the number.

On the third night she reported a second out-of-body experience. This time it was 3.35 a.m. Once again her brain waves showed an unusual pattern. Again, she failed to identify the hidden number.

On the fourth night, she had an out-of-body experience and correctly identified the number (25132). At 5.57 a.m. her brain wave recordings again showed the same unusual pattern, but this time it was more pronounced. I questioned Dr Tart about the experiment:

KP: When you did this experiment, it didn't succeed immediately, is that right?

CT: Well, it succeeded in the sense that on the first three nights she had some out-of-body experiences which gave me information about her brain waves and the like, but she didn't feel she'd been able to control her movements to see the number. On the fourth night, she reported an out-of-body experience in which she said she saw the number, and correctly reported that it was 25132.

KP: Now the obvious suggestion to make is that in some way during the night she unplugged herself from the apparatus, climbed up to look over the shelf and actually cheated by looking at the number directly. How do you answer that?

CT: Well nothing that obvious would have been possible. There are very short connections between her scalp and the brain wave apparatus, and if she had unplugged those in order to do that it would have caused tremendous agitation of the machinery that would have been perfectly obvious. So if she engaged in any kind of fraud it was very elaborately done. I don't rule it out absolutely, but personally I have no feeling that it happened.

Dr Tart does not himself consider these experiments to be crucial, particularly since he lost touch with Miss Z when she moved to another part of America. He carried out similar experiments with another subject, a business man from Virginia, but with less clear results.

Earlier, I mentioned the possibility that all paranormal effects come from one general property of the mind and matter. If I accept that Miss Z did go 'out of body' to read the number on the shelf, was it that her mind, like the hologram example, wobbled its way free of the body and went up to the shelf? Or was it that a special temporary connection or interaction occurred between her consciousness, her internal 'I' and the number on the shelf?

One of the many striking features about the out-of-body experience is that many people have reported seeing apparitions of the person having the out-of-body experience *at the place* where the person said they went *during* the experience. But this is an anecdote, and to keep to my pledge, I cannot give it more than passing reference. This does not at all mean that I discount every anecdote. There are hundreds of highly consistent accounts of these experiences and either all the people reporting them were deluded or frauds, or something very strange happened to them. Here we must look only at experiments to try and get answers.

A scientist called Blue Harary has two pet kittens called 'Spirit' and 'Soul'; he claimed that he could generate out-of-body experiences at will, but only after a prolonged and very careful period of preparation, meditation and relaxation.

He is very fond of his kittens and has a strong loving relationship with them. With some other scientists monitoring the attempt, he decided to go out-of-body to his cats, and to see whether his cat altered its behaviour in one place when his out-of-body mind reached that place.

First of all, the experimenters put Spirit in an enclosure marked out as in the picture and measured how many squares he walked over in a particular time and how many 'meows' Spirit made during the same time. Then Harary, in another building, prepared himself to go out-of-body to Spirit.

This 'cool-down' preparation period took him nearly the whole day in a specially sound-proofed room and produced a number of definite and consistent changes in the behaviour of his body and brain waves, which were measured in much the same way as those of Miss Z.

The observers who were measuring Spirit's walking and meowing were 'blind' to the actual times when Blue Harary said he went out of body, which was on average twice per session. At other times, as a comparative control, another investigator deliberately engaged Harary in conversation, to make quite sure he did *not* have an out-of-body experience at that time. Spirit's observer was also 'blind' to these times. After a large number of repeats of this experiment, they found that Spirit stopped meowing altogether

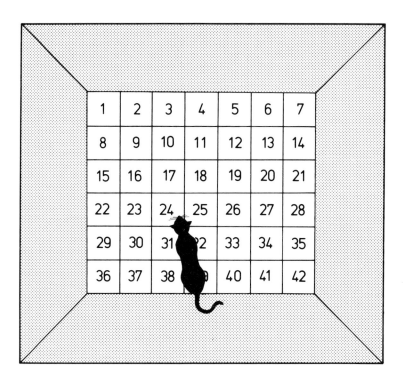

Fig. 52
Blue Harary's cat was observed walking in a room with the floor marked in squares. Harary was in another room preparing for an 'out-of-body experience'. Under double-blind conditions (the observer of the cat did not know when Harary had his experiences) the number of squares the cat walked through in a given time, and the number of miaows, were recorded. Subsequent correlation showed that when Harary said he was 'out-of-body' and 'with his cat', the cat walked about and miaowed significantly less. The experimenters did *not* conclude that Harary *was* 'out-of-body', but that there was a connection and information exchange between the cat and Harary.

[3] Quoted in N. Bowles, F. Hynds and J. Maxwell, *Psi Search*, Harper and Row, New York, 1978

and moved one hundred times less often at the times when Harary claimed he left his body to 'go', in his terms, to his cat.

We might conclude that the cat was sensitive to the presence of his disembodied mind, but that is *not* what the investigators concluded. They said, more cautiously, that there had been some information exchange between subject and animal. They concluded that although it was impossible to validate Harary's claim that his mind had left his body, events occurred at the time when he *said* he did, which suggested that there had been an interaction between man and animal. [3]

That is a very different thing from saying that an out-of-body experience *really* occurs. Once again we need to remind ourselves that the physicists are no longer talking about studying an external, objective space where things travel, but only about studying *interactions* between observers and things being observed. When our senses and common sense demand a good hard-edged 'reality' to explain these effects, the physicists will say only that the reality you discover depends partly on the experiment you perform. Therefore the best the experimenters could do with Harary and his cats was to try and find a method which revealed a *connection*:

they called the connection between person and cat an interaction where there was an exchange of *information*.

What they measured tended to confirm what Blue Harary *experienced*. Method, connection, information and experience were all well correlated.

When we were looking at the mind as if it were a hologram in the brain, however, the analogy made it look as if it was less physically fixed in the brain; so now we could perhaps approach the bizarre idea that it could actually break loose and move out of the brain of a person as something separate from physical matter. That really is the crux of the whole matter. We have been looking at the possibility that what we experience as the mind can interact with matter across space and time, so we have to ask the question: does the mind actually go out, or is there a special channel where the paranormal effect works without having to assume the conscious mind leaving the body as an entity in its own right?

If the mind can receive images across space as in the Ganzfeld experiments and if some people can use their minds to interact with others to transmit information, as in the remote viewing experiments, and if yet others can see ahead in time like Dr Schmidt's subjects, and bend metal physically like Stephen North, then one way of looking at all these apparently different effects is to assume that they are all manifestations of one single entity. This is in fact what some investigators are doing and they call the single effect: 'psi'. This new word includes telepathy, clairvoyance, psychokinesis and precognition.

All the effects we have looked at so far are weak. They do not add up to a single, massive and consistent ability. Some people are able consistently to create small positive results, but often only over long and difficult series of trials.

Professor Brian Josephson is Professor of Physics at Cambridge University. He is a Fellow of the Royal Society, and in 1973 won the Nobel Prize for physics for his work on superconduction. Superconduction is a strange loss of electrical resistance in metals when they are cooled to temperatures approaching −273°C. An electrical current set up in a ring of metal cooled to these temperatures will circulate round and round the ring for ever because there is no electrical resistance left in the metal to impede its progress. Josephson is interested in the idea that small actions can have very large effects or, as he put it: a small *signal* can produce a very large response. I asked him to explain this:

BJ: Let me give you an example of what I mean. If I say to you, 'Pass the salt, please', then you hear my voice and you pass the salt. The energy in the sound of my voice is a very small amount of energy and it became amplified into a much larger effect. I am very interested in the relation between the two.

KP: A small sound signal produces the actual movement of a lump of metal?

BJ: Yes.

KP: But this is on a large scale. What about on a smaller scale in the atoms of the metal? Is it possible that the same sort of thing could occur there?

BJ: If something can happen on one scale, in physics it can happen on any other. So, in principle, yes, it can happen there as well.

KP: But what you seem to be saying, if I've got it right, is that your will moved the salt cellar. Are you talking about the will or the mind of somebody having an effect on atoms; is that conceivable within the realm of physics?

BJ: It's conceivable, yes.

KP: Do you think that it's actually a part of physics that this could happen?

BJ: I think it's quite possible and it's just that physicists haven't got round to thinking about it and dealing with it mathematically yet.

So it is possible that the effect on Blue Harary's cat was a very small signal having a larger effect on the behaviour of a whole animal, perhaps like a tiny pebble rippling the whole surface of a pond.

The cat experiment suggests a paranormal connection between a human mind and an animal and so the next logical question to ask is whether an out-of-body experience inside the mind of a subject could produce a physical effect exactly where the subject said he was when he went out-of-body.

Alex Tanous is a slim wiry American with an air of concentrated internal intensity. He talks rapidly and easily, but my strong impression is that he speaks from a reflective centre which he protects. He is acutely sensitive to the responses of people, and is a serious and attentive conversationalist.

Since childhood Alex has been subject to out-of-body experiences which he has described in a book. [4] Now after concentration and meditation he claims to have the experiences voluntarily.

[4] A. Tanous, *Beyond Concidence: One Man's Experience with Psychic Phenomena*, Doubleday, New York, 1976

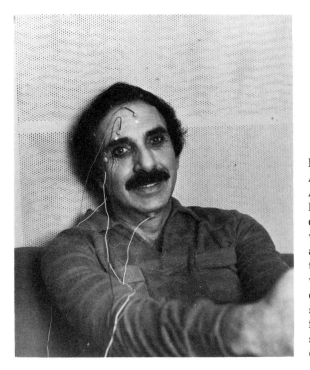

Fig. 53
Alex Tanous, the
American subject of Dr
Karlis Osis's
experiments to test
whether or not there is
a physical presence at
the observation site
when a sensitive goes
out-of-body. He is
shown here wired up
for e.e.g. recordings,
such as is done in the
experiments.

Dr Karlis Osis is an experimental psychologist and has been working on different aspects of the paranormal for many years. He is also interested in out-of-body experiences and has been experimenting with another sensitive, Ingo Swann, who also claimed to experience these strange episodes.

Osis put Swann in a laboratory again with attached electrodes to monitor his brain waves and other physiological states. A target for Swann to 'visit' was then randomly selected and put into an open-topped box suspended near the ceiling of the laboratory. Swann could not see the object as it was put into the box. He was then asked to identify the object. Eight experiments were done and then descriptions and drawings made by Swann together with the actual identity of the object were submitted to an external judge not involved in the experiment who was asked to match description with object 'blind'. All eight descriptions were correctly matched with the actual object description. This result has odds against it occurring by chance of 40,000 to 1.

Although this result took Dr Osis a step forward, he was still unable to decide whether Ingo Swann was using remote viewing plus an hallucination of leaving his body, or whether he had identified the object while his mind had actually left his body.

The problem Dr Osis faced was how to find evidence of a real 'something' leaving the body and whether that something had any position or substance. So, far, there was some evidence of a connection between the mind of Miss Z and the hidden number, Blue Harary and his kitten and Ingo Swann with the hidden object. The question now to be answered was whether someone *outside* the mind of the subject could observe a something in a particular place outside the mind of the subject while they experienced being out-of-body. This is what he did:

Fig. 54
A diagram of Dr Osis's apparatus. The projector creates a composite picture of coloured quadrant and image. Only in one point in space (the 'box') can the correct composite be identified (colour, quadrant position and image). Later, a real box was built around the 'box' in space, with two plates suspended inside with strain gauges attached. If a subject reports an out-of-body experience, and some element of the subject's mind is actually in the box, the strain gauges might register its presence.

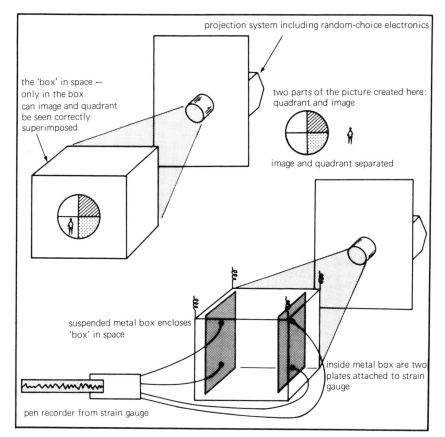

projection system including random-choice electronics

the 'box' in space — only in the box can image and quadrant be seen correctly superimposed

two parts of the picture created here: quadrant and image

image and quadrant separated

suspended metal box encloses 'box' in space

inside metal box are two plates attached to strain gauge

pen recorder from strain gauge

Inside a special slide projector he put a random series of pictures each made up of two images. One was a revolving disc divided into four quadrants, each of a different colour, and the other was a familiar picture outline like a shoe or a fish arranged so that the picture could be superimposed on any one of the four quadrants. It could, therefore, appear at upper left, lower left, upper right or lower right.

If the picture of a fish appeared on the lower left quadrant and the lower left quadrant was blue, the correct identification of the picture would be: 'Fish, blue, lower left quadrant.' Any other description would be wrong in one or more component parts of the image.

Dr Osis then built another machine so that the image, the colour and the position of the whole target picture were all selected and then mixed at random by a small computer. For each assembled picture there were obviously a large number of permutations and these could be exactly calculated.

He then began to experiment. Alex Tanous was shut in a sound-proof chamber, where he began to relax and get himself into the right internal condition to have an out-of-body experience. Again his brain and body were wired up to physiological recording electrodes to register his general bodily condition. Then Osis asked him to try and project his mind into the laboratory where the projector apparatus was housed and to try and make a correct identification of the picture inside the apparatus.

The ingenious catch in the experiment was this. The whole picture could only be seen from one particular position in space. From any other viewpoint, it was impossible to superimpose picture on colour or quadrant. So, if Alex Tanous's mind was truly out of his body, his 'mind' had to be in a particular 'place' to see correctly. If his 'mind' was in any other position, he could not identify the picture correctly at all, because its various components (quadrant, position, colour and picture) could not all be seen together in their correct inter-relationship.

What Dr Osis found was that Tanous did in fact achieve a significant number of correct whole-image identifications in a large number of experiments. Nevertheless there were still doubts, even if Tanous was 'remotely viewing' the whole picture from the correct position in space. The experiment did not establish that there was a particular 'entity' actually at the only position in space where the whole picture could be correctly viewed.

Osis then reasoned that if Tanous's mind had any physical presence at the correct viewing position, then it might be possible to set up very sensitive detecting instruments around the position to try and detect a physical presence at the same time as Tanous said he was there: in effect, a 'mind detector'.

Osis used strain gauges like those which Professor Hasted used to detect the bending of metals. He first built a shielded metal box around the 'place' where the picture could be successfully identified and then arranged instruments to detect any disturbance of the strain gauges attached to the walls of the box. He reasoned that if Tanous's mind left his body and 'went' to the only place where the picture could be identified, the entity of his mind might set off the strain gauges.

Fig. 55
A picture of part of the lab in which the out-of-body experiments are conducted, taken during the filming for the series. Dr Osis is seated; the author stands behind, and the film camera partly obscures the e.e.g. recording apparatus.

[5] K. Osis and D. McCormick, *Journal of the American Society of Psychical Research*, vol. 74, 1980

Dr Osis is still in the middle of these experiments (December 1980) and is very cautious about the results. He is fully aware of their totally unprecedented nature. Up to now what he has found is that there is a small but definite connection between successful whole-image identification by Tanous and the times when the strain gauges give a signal, suggesting that some 'thing' or entity goes into the box when Tanous makes his identification and the 'thing' is to do with Tanous's mind. As I write this, Dr Osis has just published the first account of his experiments [5], and we will certainly have to wait until they are repeated by someone else before anything more definite can be said.

If these experiments on out-of-body experience develop and show a greater degree of consistency and significance, there is no doubt at all that they will have helped to solve one of the most difficult problems that we have faced: whether there is an entity called mind and whether this is separable from the physical body. It is tantalising, because, as Dr Osis himself has written, his results are so unprecedented that they must be confirmed by the other investigators before their conclusions find more general acceptance.

Miss Z, Blue Harary and Alex Tanous all seem to be specially gifted people, but now I want to see whether paranormal abilities are more general in the public at large and whether particular types of personality do better than others.

11. Sheep, Goats and Philip

Dr Gertrude Schmeidler has a warm but quizzical way of looking at you. As you talk with her and she begins to warm to the conversation and overcome a natural shyness, you realise you are engaged with a profoundly knowledgeable and charmingly elliptical intelligence. She is constantly on the look-out for new ways of interpreting apparently simple human traits, and without any sense that you are an experimental subject you eventually realise that the conversation you are holding is under friendly but wise scrutiny. She has spent much of her professional life as an experimental psychologist in examining the personality traits and character types associated with paranormal ability. One of her early experiments was so unlikely in design, I found it hard to digest when I first talked with her about it.

She was working with a group of students in a New York college and gave each one a form to fill. On the form, there were questions to the effect: do you believe in extra-sensory perception, do you find it possible or, do you disbelieve it? Then an astonishing second instruction: I [Dr Schmeidler] am going to turn up randomised cards in a certain order *tomorrow morning* and I would like you now (today) to write down your predictive guess as to the order in which they will appear. The forms were filled, the predictions made and the results assessed. Those who wrote that they accepted e.s.p. scored significantly better at predicting the order of the cards than those who wrote that they did not believe it. [1]

She called the believers who did better 'sheep', and the disbelievers who did worse 'goats' – sheep because they accepted the challenge to exhibit paranormal activity and goats because they resisted the challenge. This has since become known as the 'sheep-goat effect' and has been widely repeated with very similar results. [2]

Dr Schmeidler then went on to use a particular system of personality testing to establish the degree of adjustment of e.s.p. subjects. The tests included the Rorschach technique and other related methods. The Rorschach test involves asking the subject to

[1] G. Schmeidler and R. McConnell, *ESP and Personality Patterns*, Yale University Press, 1958

[2] J. Palmer, *Journal of the American Society for Psychical Research*, vol. 66, 1972 (two articles)

[3] J. Randall,
Parapsychology and
the Nature of Life,
Abacus, London, 1977

[4] M. R. Barrington,
Journal of the Society
for Psychical Research,
vol. 47, 1973

[5] H. Eysenck,
Journal of the Society
for Psychical Research,
vol. 44, 1967

[6] B. Kanthamani and
K. Rao, Journal of
Parapsychology, vol.
36, 1972

[7] R. Smith and B.
Humphrey, Journal of
Parapsychology, vol.
10, 1946

[8] G. Caspar, Journal
of Parapsychology,
vol. 16, 1952

[9] D. Busby, Journal
of Parapsychology,
vol. 31, 1967

[10] M. Johnson and
B. Kanthamani,
Journal of
Parapsychology, vol.
31, 1967

interpret what pictures they see in randomly made ink patterns. Dr Schmeidler found that the best adjusted subjects achieved the highest deviation from chance and the poorly adjusted subjects, whether sheep or goats, did badly.

These tests suggested an interesting division between the *amount* of e.s.p. ability and the *direction* of e.s.p. ability: [3] the *amount* depending on social adjustment and the *direction* upon belief.

Since Gertrude Schmeidler's original work, the psychological and personality characters of e.s.p. have been analysed and examined in very great detail and there is probably a more profuse literature on this aspect of the paranormal than any other. For example, one English investigator, M. R. Barrington, [4] divided subjects into four groups: moderate believers, uncertain but inclined to believe, unconvinced, doubtful. There were no absolute sheep or goats in the group. As expected, the e.s.p. results matched in descending order with the degree of acceptance of e.s.p.

Another psychologist, Hans Eysenck, compared personality type and paranormal ability in a slightly different way by looking for signs of what he termed 'extraversion' and 'neuroticism'. He was able to demonstrate that a majority of subjects with a high paranormal ability tended to be extroverted rather than introverted. Or, more simply, outgoing people did better than the more reserved. [5]

Another study with schoolchildren confirmed that extroverts were better at e.s.p. than introverts at odds against chance producing the difference of 20,000 to 1. [6]

The way people sketch and draw has also been related to paranormal abilities. One investigator found that people who drew 'expansively' did better than people who made small, compressed sketches. [7]

Another study revealed that in telepathy experiments, extrovert 'receivers' did better than introvert 'receivers' who tended to achieve below chance or 'psi-missing' results. [8] Also, subjects who view the world in a holistic way (see page 11) did better than people who analysed it in a reductionist manner (see page 11). [9] People with a low level of general anxiety, as measured by the Defense Mechanism Test, did better than people with a high level. [10]

There is a detailed literature of this type of relationship between personality and e.s.p. ability, and what emerges fairly clearly is that expansive, calm, friendly people tend to do better than inward-looking, anxious and reserved people.

I put this to Dr Schmeidler that nice people did better and, as you might expect, I got a ticking off for being simplistic:

Oh no, it's not nearly so simple as that, there's much more to it. For example, two scientists decided to do a long-term piece of research looking for good subjects, and under very careful conditions they tested a very large group, but the tests meant that the subjects had to leave home during evenings and weekends and their wives resented it. The experimenters kept on getting chance results, chance results, chance results from their subjects until their wives said, how about trying us? And when the wives came and were tested the wives got very high scores. Now, the experimenters, I think, were very 'nice', to use your word, but the wives, even in that formal situation, saw through any barriers of stiffness and formality, and experimental correctness and saw the 'niceness' of the investigators, whereas the subjects who had grown familiar with them didn't see them at all.

I then asked her about her most recent work connecting paranormal ability and personality. She had in fact turned the tables and experimented on the experimenters themselves:

We were given permission very graciously by twenty people who were talking at the Paris Psychological Convention [in 1979] to take video tapes of them while they were making their prepared remarks at the Convention and also while they were waiting for questions from the audience and then responding to those questions.

Among those people there was a batch that had been getting no results again and again, quite consistently; their subjects just had not been showing e.s.p. and there were quite a few others, whose subjects had consistently been showing e.s.p. We paired the two groups on the basis of age, sex, and other variables.

We made five-minute segments of film of each speaker and then showed the segments without any sound, so all that the viewing students could see were gestures and facial expressions, so they got a little feeling of tempo. Then we asked the students to rate each of these twenty people on thirty different adjectives that relate to personality. And when we looked at the differences between the subjects who got good scores and those who got poor ones, we found that they were statistically significant for 14 out of the 30 adjectives. The experimenters who had been getting no results were rated more rigid, more tense and more egoistic. I'm sure the ratings were wrong, the people weren't really egoistic, it's just that they came through this way – perhaps from excessive shyness and over compensation. The people who had been getting more positive e.s.p. results had ratings showing them significantly more flexible, more enthusiastic, freer, and more likeable.

This is perhaps one of the best examples of what is known among researchers as the 'experimenter effect', which means that the experimenter can be shown experimentally to be part of the experiment and to affect its outcome. This is no more than current physics in saying: that the experiment designed by the experimenter controls the outcome of the experiment. The experimenter effect is well known to ordinary psychologists, [11] and is sometimes called 'demand bias' or 'demand characteristic'.[12] What it means is that the experimenter, usually unconsciously, makes his subjects behave in a way that will cause them to get results which will come out in accordance with his expectations – or, more crudely, they tend consciously or unconsciously to brainwash their subjects. Helmudt Schmidt, for example, told some of his subjects working with his random number machines that they were not succeeding and they actually began to achieve 'psi-missing' or below chance results. With another group, he consistently encouraged his subjects to believe that they were doing well, and they achieved better and better results.

The real problem for researchers to overcome here is realizing that they may not be discovering a real property of the outside world, but only the effect of their view of it on others.

The net result of work on the 'experimenter effect' is to show that a 'sheep' experimenter may achieve positive results and a 'goat' experimenter may get negative results while performing exactly similar experiments. Unfortunately, this very real effect has evoked considerable bitterness and anger in literature on the paranormal. If a 'goat' experimenter decides to repeat the same experiment as a 'sheep' experimenter and gets negative results, he commonly accuses the 'sheep' of fraud or bad experiment. Fortunately there are 'sheep' experimenters who also produce negative experimenter bias and who are also generous enough to recognise the problem. Dr John Beloff is one such investigator who, although he accepts that some paranormal effects are genuine, himself consistently gets negative experimental results. So he is a 'sheep' who consistently gets 'goat' effects, but has the scientific honesty to record the matter.

Another complicating factor about the psychology of experiments on the paranormal is what is known as the 'decline effect'. When a gifted subject starts work, he or she may do spectacularly

[11] R. Rosenthal, *Experimenter Effects in Behavioural Research*, Appleton-Century-Crofts, New York, 1966

[12] M. Orne, *American Psychologist*, vol. 17, 1962

well for a while, but then the results slowly drop away down to a chance level. People I have spoken to in the field seem generally agreed that this could really be called the 'boredom effect'. If someone is asked just to press buttons day after day in a laboratory situation for no advantage or reward, it is not really surprising that whatever mental faculty paranormal ability is eventually falls asleep.

The published psychological evidence on paranormal ability suggests strongly that it is a 'people-orientated' effect and here, I think, lies one of the principal causes of disagreement between other scientists and experimenters on the paranormal.

One of the main canons of the scientific method is that every experiment should be repeatable – an entirely reasonable position. If all the methods and details of an experiment are published, then another investigator should be able to get the same results.

If I punch a hole in three separate pieces of card and arrange them so that a ray of light goes through all three holes and strikes a screen, I record a spot of light on the screen. If I displace one of the pieces of card, the spot of light on the screen disappears and so I conclude that the ray of light travels in a straight line. Another experimenter repeating this will get the same result and another and another and so on.

Paranormal effects seem to be definite, but small, delicate and very much related to the mental state of the subject, and so it is not a real repetition of experimental method if another, perhaps a 'goat' experimenter, says to a subject: 'Please come to my laboratory at 8.30 on Monday morning and repeat the successful experiments you did with my "sheep" colleague.' The 'goat' would first have to reproduce the mental rapport achieved by his sheep colleague. Doctrinaire positions of this sort are becoming much less common among scientists, as more of them tend to accept that the paranormal is a valid area for investigation. And the evidence?

Dr Christopher Evans was an old friend of mine and now, alas, he has died at a very early age. He is perhaps best known as presenter and writer of the television series *The Mighty Micro*. Chris was sternly opposed to the whole area of the paranormal and wrote that it was 'a relic of the past with an aura of faded pre-war newspapers, the Graf Zeppelin and the Entente Cordiale'. [13]

[13] C. Evans, *New Scientist*, vol. 41, 1969

Then the *New Scientist*, with the collaboration of Chris, carried out a survey of whether its mainly scientist readers accepted the paranormal or not. Out of 1,500 replies received, 25 per cent stated that they regarded e.s.p. as established, 42 per cent thought that it was likely; only 3 per cent thought it to be impossible.

[14] C. Evans, *New Scientist*, vol. 57, 1973

[15] A. Gresley, *The Sociology of the Paranormal*, Saga Publications, California, 1975

With characteristic forthrightness and clarity, Chris then declared that '... the stated opinion of nearly 1,500 readers, the majority of whom are working scientists and technologists on a topic as controversial as parapsychology cannot be lightly dismissed. Clearly a large number of serious scientists consider it to be a highly interesting and potentially immensely significant branch of science.' [14]

In 1975 an American sociologist, Andrew Greely, carried out a survey of about 1,400 people carefully chosen to be a representative cross-section of the population as a whole. His object was to discover what percentage of people had experienced paranormal events. Of the sample, 58 per cent reported telepathic experience, 32 per cent felt that they had experienced telepathy several times, and 24 per cent reported one or more clairvoyant episodes. Further, 10 per cent had had several clairvoyant experiences, 27 per cent believed that they had been in contact with the dead once and 11 per cent believed they had done so several times. [15]

As I write this *The Times* has just published (20 December 1980) the result of a questionnaire it put to its readers. This is given in full as Appendix IV. Of 1,314 replies received, 64 per cent believe that psychic experiences exist, 83 per cent accept e.s.p. in general, 83 per cent accept telepathy and 73 per cent accept precognition.

So far I have been looking at individual subjects working with a single investigator. Many psychologists believe that group experiences can exert more powerful effects. So now I am going to look at a particular group experience of the paranormal which apparently produced something entirely unexpected.

If you look at Fig. 56, you can see a group of people with their hands on a table which is apparently floating in the air. But, going back to the rules of evidence which I opened with in Chapter 1, there is no active evidence in the picture to show that the table is floating. The photograph is a still from a film made by Canadian television and when the film is viewed as a whole, the table does indeed appear to be floating while the group surrounding it keep their hands on its top surface.

One of my earlier warnings was 'do not believe what you see'. Professor Ellison was able to levitate a bowl of flowers by ordinary magnetic means, and yet two observers swore that they saw two entirely different things happen. What is worse, it is perfectly simple to make it appear that a table with hands firm placed on top of it is floating round a room. There are many other ways of doing it, which are no more than first-grade studies for any self-respecting conjurer.

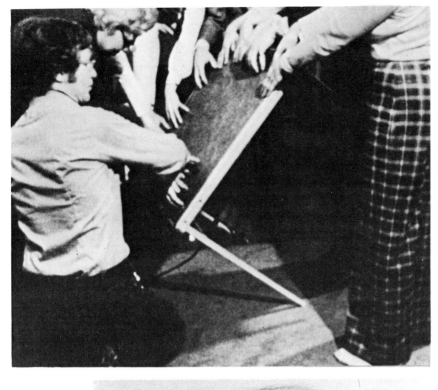

Fig. 56
A still from the 'Philip' film. Stills are not convincing, since all one sees is a group of people 'holding a table'. However, the motion the film shows would be difficult to fake, and this still is taken from a point in the film where the table remains motionless for two or three seconds, tipped over. Notice that the hands on the right side of the table are scarcely in contact. It's not particularly convincing; the film, however, seen as a whole, is more so, and it should be remembered that the session was conducted with continual observation, so that collusion or fakery is reasonably well excluded. A film alone, however, can never be accepted as evidence of a paranormal event.

Fig. 57
Philip, as drawn by one of the team members, from the story they collectively devised.

So what has the film got to do with the creation of real external happenings with the mind?

The people around the table in fact decided a long time before the film was made to meet regularly as a group and try to *create* a ghost. You are quite entitled to ask at this stage whether they did it with butter muslin and luminous paint!

What they had decided was that psychokinesis was such a wayward and difficult effect for an individual to achieve that they would try to make something happen as a group. So they invented 'Philip'.

Philip, their creation, is a good-looking young man, an aristocrat living in the time of Cromwell in 1600. He was married to a beautiful but unloving wife Dorothea and then fell hopelessly in love with a raven-haired gypsy called Margo. Dorothea eventually found out about Margo, accused her of witchcraft and had her burnt at the stake. Bear with me a little longer.

Philip, in despair, finally flung himself from the battlements and was killed. All of which is first-class B-movie material. And that, as a matter of fact, is exactly what it was. Philip was a *total* invention: mediaeval ham drama with all the trimmings. Philip had *no* historical validity; *no* basis in reality and *no* existence whatever. He was the brain-child of one of a group of eight people who decided they would get together and try to 'will' Philip into existence. For almost a year, the group met every week for about two hours to see whether ordinary people could generate some sort of spirit or ghost, and if they could discover whether it was disembodied spirit or some manifestation of themselves. The attempt was absolutely serious, although Philip was pure costume melodrama.

The group comprised an engineer, an accountant, an industrial designer, a scientific research assistant, and four housewives. None claimed to be a medium and all were of a sceptical turn of mind and wanted to see whether their collective effort would turn out to have an external and real result, or whether it would be revealed as a group hallucination.

The reason why they invented the fictitious character of Philip was to give them the opportunity of being more lighthearted than is usual in most experiments. Far from being a gruelling, concentrated and serious effort, the creation of Philip became a game to be played for fun: the Philip game.

Paranormal events often seem to occur when the concentration of the experimental subject is relaxed. Subjects like Stephen North work hard for a long time on a particular task and then, just as they stop, something paranormal happens.

How can anyone possibly invent someone who never existed? It seems to be a complete contradiction in terms. And it is, but what the group tried to do was to use the completely fictitious idea of Philip to somehow give themselves *permission* to do something extraordinary. They began by meditating together often around a sketch of Philip and they would discuss Philip's appearance and the affairs of his spurious family. Gradually, the saga of the non-existent Philip grew and became more detailed.

At the end of a full year of weekly meetings, absolutely nothing had happened and they talked of giving up. The one positive result which they had achieved was that they all come to know one another very well and had achieved close bonds of affection and friendship. Then they discovered the work of some English experimenters who had tried something similar several years previously, [16] and who believed that paranormal phenomena are not caused by mysterious effects peculiar to gifted people called psychics or mediums, but are essentially *psychological skills* which can be learnt by absolutely everyone. Having read the results of the English experimenters, the 'Philip' group decided to re-convene and to change their tactics.

[16] K. J. Batcheldor, *Journal of the Society for Psychical Research*, vol. 43, 1966

The alterations they made were mainly in their own attitudes to the task. They still wanted to produce a materialisation of Philip, but now they worked more at relaxing. They sang songs together until they were no longer embarrassed by singing badly; they told rather weak jokes and generally tried to quell their doubts and to believe that they could produce Philip. On the third or fourth of the new sessions they all felt and then heard raps on the table, and then the raps got louder and finally the table itself began to move.

What do we have? A group of people who, by their own admission, want to believe in what they are trying to do, and lo and behold it happens. The very worst sort of anecdote. As a matter of fact, they agreed with this diagnosis. The onset of the raps created some suspicion among themselves. Each member thought someone else in the group was hitting the table or kicking it with their foot. This is a very reasonable idea. The most suspicious thing of all was that they then learnt, as a group, to communicate with Philip with the raps. One rap meant 'yes' and two raps meant 'no', in the most indulgent of spiritualist tradition.

Then the table started to move round the room and to levitate. So now it appeared that not only had they learnt to communicate with a completely non-existent character called 'Philip' by raps on the table, but that the table was also moving around the room. Just the sort of story we want to avoid. All that's missing is a crystal ball and ghostly music.

After 'communication' with the wholly fictitious Philip had evolved and developed, all the members of the group took increasing pains to remove possibilities of fraud or self-deception. They were obsessed with the obvious accusation: 'You must somehow be doing it yourselves, either consciously or unconsciously.'

However, the raps and the table movements went on happening in good lighting and often in the presence of highly sceptical scientist visitors who were looking for nudges, kicks and other ways of moving the table normally. Finally the 'Philip' effects were produced in front of television lights and cameras.

That still does not show clearly enough that Philip was created from nothing. One other feature helps. There were in fact some peculiar qualities about the raps and the moving of the table which Dr Lawrence Le Shan (see page 26) actually witnessed. Dr Le Shan was present at several of the Philip sessions and heard the raps on the table and their transference to a metal sheet suspended by some cords directly above the table. He also heard the raps coming from the metal. I talked to him about what he saw.

KP: Dr Le Shan you were present when Philip manifested himself. What did you yourself personally witness?

LLS: I personally witnessed the rappings on the table. The group were sitting around a table with a rather light surface; it was not a thick surface. I was then asked if I wanted to say hello to Philip and I put my hand on the table and said, 'Hello, Philip,' at which point there was a very sharp clear rap right under my hand. I watched this, using the usual precautions one takes when dealing with fake mediums and conjurers and so forth; skills which every psychologist has to learn. It seemed pretty plain to me that none of the people there was doing this.

KP: This is very important, because there are lots of ways of rapping on a table and I'm sure you know as many of them as I do. Are you really sure there was nobody rapping the table with a finger or kicking the leg, or anything like that?

LLS: There is very little question this was a very clear phenomenon. And there are two other reasons for also believing it to be a clear phenomenon; one is that at one point the metal plate was lowered to about eighteen inches above the table; no one was touching it, no one was near it.

KP: It was suspended on strings, wasn't it?

LLS: It was suspended on four strings one from each corner, and exactly the size of the surface of the table.

KP: And you had a clear view all round it?

LLS: A clear view all round. There was simply no one there and I'm reasonably certain there was no one with an air rifle shooting pellets at it from a far corner! When the plate came down to within eighteen inches of the table, the table stopped rattling and the plate began to 'ping'. I spent quite some time afterwards trying to reproduce that pinging myself getting the same kind of sound, but I had no success. This was a very clear phenomenon, no one was touching the plate or near it. I'm sure this was not conjuring.

KP: And you're quite certain that the 'ping' on the plate was something inside the plate, not a sound that's say projected on to it by some electronic device?

LLS: I'm quite certain of this; I've had a fair amount of experience with conjuring and I also have to say in terms of my own attitude that I'd much prefer that it *was* a trick. I'm *not* happy with psychokinesis, with this kind of manifestation of psychokinetic ability. My own peace of mind would have been greater if I could have found a trick.

KP: Did you know the Philip group?

LLS: I knew the Philip people quite well.

KP: What sort of people were they?

LLS: Dr George Owen is one of the most reliable people in the whole field. He's a mathematician, a geneticist and was a Professor at Cambridge in both subjects. A serious and dedicated man.

KP: So you don't feel in any way they're up to some collective trick?

LLS: No. It's simply beyond question.

As time went on, the Philip group learned more skills; they produced raps in other parts of the room and on some occasions the table moved of its own volition. It began to look as if they were running a self-teaching class in how to do the paranormal. Many people who have studied this type of phenomenon think very much like that also.

One English investigator wrote:

...the production of paranormal physical phenomena is a kind of skill which appears to be subject to the laws of learning; simple procedures have to be followed. As with professional skills ... success is achieved by learning, example, practice, aptitude and experience. A step-by-step advance from simple and more plausible paranormal tasks is indicated. Belief and expectancy then snowball. [17]

[17] C. Brookes Smith and D. Hunt, *Journal of the Society for Psychical Research*, vol. 47, 1973

It is the 'belief and expectancy' part that it is so difficult for science to accept. It sounds too much like the already converted trying to enhance their beliefs by auto-suggestion. However, if the effects they produce are *externally* verifiable and there is freedom from gullibility and fraud, I have to accept that a non-existent, invented B-movie character was actually conjured up out of thin air and not that the group just experienced a group hallucination, or collective self-delusion. The objective, external evidence of the raps is strong.

The most plausible explanation of 'Philip' is that the 'Philip game' allowed the group to be childlike and adopt an ingénue game-playing attitude and to develop their own psychokinetic abilities without heavy adult overlay. They did not so much create Philip, but exteriorised their own minds as a group experience so that they could produce external physical events. Another way of saying this would be that the Philip group generated their own poltergeist.

The history of poltergeists or 'noise spirits', as the word means, goes back a long way. For example, as early as 858, at Bingen in Germany, stones were flying about in the air, and at the home of one William Not in Wales, lumps of dirt were flying through the air and clothing was tearing spontaneously. This is all very well, since these are all historical anecdotes and inadmissible according to our rules. The poltergeist reports, however, are so similar to the Philip event, and there have simply been so many accounts of similar happenings, that it would be impossible to ignore the anecdotes altogether. What is more, as Alan Gauld of Nottingham University and others are beginning to show, poltergeist phenomena are capable of being investigated by rational experimentation. [18]

[18] A. Gauld and A. Cornell, *Poltergeists*, Routledge and Kegan Paul, London, Boston, Henley, 1979

[19] W. Roll, *The Poltergeist*, Scarecrow Press, Metuchen, New Jersey, 1976

Another very experienced investigator of poltergeists now suggests that some 'lawfulness' in poltergeist reports is beginning to emerge. [19] Movements of flying objects, for example, seem to have consistent patterns and sequences.

Assuming that the Philip experience is genuine, and I see no good reason to doubt it, we have an apparent connection between mind or, in this case, a group of minds, and matter. This may turn out to be the most likely explanation of the poltergeist, rather than having to assume the more untidy idea that a poltergeist is a disembodied spirit.

When I first heard of the Philip story, I am bound to confess that I was strongly biased against it, simply because the whole structure of the event and story seemed to be so enormously unlikely. Now, having studied it and talked with people who were directly involved, I am prepared to accept that a group of sceptical people did, by group effort, interaction and experience, generate physical effects.

One of the group who actually invented the story of Philip commented:

At the beginning of the Philip experiment I was probably the greatest sceptic of the group. The main objective was to create a visible thought-form by using the combined subconscious thoughts from a group of ordinary people.

My scepticism was strengthened by my certain knowledge, having created the story, that Philip had never existed. Others in the group could search for ways he could be real, but I knew he was only a product of my imagination.

By the end of the first year I was astonished at the closeness of the bond which had formed among the members of the group. They were people with diversified interests, none being similar to mine, and they had become very dear friends. The telepathic bond between us had also become very strong. Once the table-moving and raps phenomena began, my scepticism grew greatly. I found myself watching almost obsessively for any sign of fraud. We all realise that at times we subconsciously moved with the table. However, I would now state definitely that the movement is without effort on our part, and the raps have no known physical explanation.

The experiment is a continuing one. We are still trying to manifest a thought-form, and having once had the table off the floor, we are aiming for the ceiling. We have caused knocks to happen at a distance at a given time, and we hope to be able to move objects, as in the common poltergeist phenomena. The inferences of the importance of this experiment boggle the mind. Here is a source of energy which, if investigated and developed, could be used to benefit mankind.

In the end, interpretation of events like Philip boil down to what is known among scientists as 'Occam's Razor'. William of Occam was probably born around 1300 at Ockham in Surrey, and during a varied and often pugnacious anti-clerical career he began to cast doubt on many theological assumptions. He effectively said to the clerics, 'Don't talk to me about gods in heaven; they are all in your heads.' Niels Bohr would have enjoyed this statement as pre-empting complementarity, since Occam was proposing a second view of the gods.

Joseph Campbell, the mythographer, points out with great insight that with one sweep of his razor, Occam turned metaphysics into psychology. [20] Occam actually wrote: 'Entia non sunt multiplicanda praeter necessitatem', or, 'Entities are not to be multiplied except from necessity'. This is widely misquoted by scientists. It may even have not been written as such by him at all. But he did write: 'It is vain to do with more what can be done with fewer.' Both statements add up to Occam's Razor which really means: the minimum necessary ideas are enough if they explain the subject being analysed.

So with the story of Philip: what is the minimum necessary idea? That the Philip group collectively deluded themselves and massively defrauded large numbers of the public, or that collectively they were able to produce a psychokinetic effect? In my view there is more evidence for the latter than there is for the former. Further, there is nothing in the tenets of the new physics that is either doctrinally against such a happening or says that it is impossible.

The people concerned in the Philip affair have now written about the experience in detail. [21] In the introduction, Dr George Owen, the geneticist referred to by Dr Le Shan, described the affair as 'Psychokinesis by committee'.

Many people who have shown experimentally verifiable paranormal ability have become increasingly impatient with the business. They cannot see the point of continuing to press buttons, guess cards or predict events. Their collective comment seems to be, 'I know I can do it, so why do the scientists keep on devising these boring and trivial experiments to prove that I have this ability? I would much rather know how I can use it to help people.' So now I want to look at people who do claim to apply their gifts to help others by paranormal means, the healers.

[20] J. Campbell, *The Masks of God*, Condor Books, London, 1976

[21] I. Owen and M. Sparrow, *Conjuring Up Philip*, Harper and Row, New York, 1976

12. Healers, Hands and Doctors

It was years after I had qualified as a medical doctor before I realised that I had been subjected to a six-year-long conditioning process. I had been turned out of medical school as an efficient medical and surgical technician, but woefully bereft as a healer.

It is not that the skills I had been taught were wrong or inadequate, quite the reverse. Conventional medicine is powerful and, within its own limits, highly effective, and I am delighted to pay tribute to it here by recording that I owe my life directly to a number of highly skilled and entirely conventional doctors and surgeons. (James, Tom and Stanley, thank you.) Conventional medicine is sometimes called 'allopathy' or treatment by opposites. The word is the reverse of 'homeopathy' which is treatment by small doses producing the same symptoms. In practice, 'allopathy' is just used to mean conventional medicine.

The conditioning process I had been subjected to as a student had convinced me absolutely that anyone without a medical degree came under the dreaded and damning label of 'quack'. (The *Oxford Dictionary* is regally abusive about a 'quack': 'Ignorant pretender to skills ... one who offers wonderful remedies or devices, charlatan.') It was a long time before I realised the truth that there were indeed a large number of 'quacks', but about half of them were medically qualified.

No single group of people should be able to operate a monopoly on health, but, by the same token, no one should be able to claim to heal without having to prove their claim.

There are, unfortunately, a large number of people, some of whom are medical doctors and others not, who do not seem to understand the basic ground rules of either evidence or reason, and who spend much of their life in deluding the ailing public either for prestige or profit. You can find all varieties in Harley Street if you do not trip over a Rolls-Royce.

However, this book is about the effect of mind on matter. So the first question I want to ask here is: 'Can the mind of a healer, qualified or not, affect the matter of the body of a sick patient?' If this does happen: 'Is the effect due to the rapport and relationship between healer and patient, or is there a separable and paranormal mind-over-matter effect at work as well?' An electronic box can be connected to the finger of a patient and can measure some electrical properties of the skin called the galvanic skin response, or g.s.r. (see page 54. The g.s.r is related to the level of anxiety or relaxation in the patient and changes with alteration in either of those two states in a matter of a second or two. It works by measuring changes in the electrical resistance of skin, which is altered both by sweat and the diameter of the blood vessels.)

Various machines like it have now been built and tested and they are all grouped together under the heading of 'biofeedback machines', and this means only that you can get some external feedback of how your *internal* mind-body state is.

The g.s.r. response is often linked to a loudspeaker, so that state of arousal or relaxation is converted into a series of clicks. This does not mean that your mind-body is clicking, but that your mind-body state is being played back in the form of clicks. The faster the train of clicks, the more aroused or anxious you are, and the slower the train of clicks, the more relaxed you are.

I have spent many interesting hours 'listening' to my internal state in this way and it is quite easy, after a while, to learn how to quieten yourself down by making the clicks get slower. I began to pride myself on this ability until my youngest son managed to do it about three times faster. In a matter of a few seconds, he had converted a stream of clicks rapid enough to make a musical note down to a series of occasional clicks, one every second or so. Perhaps we lose abilities when we grow up. Biofeedback machines have now become quite complicated, and people have learnt to control their heart rate, their blood pressure and, to a limited extent, their electrical brain waves or e.e.g.

In each case a mechanical loop is created. The loop goes from mind to body, to finger, to machine, to loudspeaker, to ear and back to mind again. It is true to say that, for the time when the machine is attached, a new temporary creature is assembled, a transient bionic man, with the mind freely able to range through body and machine at will. There is, however, nothing paranormal about biofeedback; it just creates a new control circuit for the owner of the body to make changes in the body which he would not otherwise be able to do.

Where the control of the brain waves by the mind inside the brain is concerned, something more interesting is going on. For here is the mind inside the brain looking at the electrical behaviour of the brain and altering that behaviour. The mind is directly affecting the matter of the brain so that the electrical activity of that matter is altered. Thus you could then argue that the changed matter of the brain is re-affecting the mind.

Someone could object and say instead: 'You are not doing that; what you are doing is to alter the *behaviour* of the brain.' To this I would retort that the behaviour of the physical brain must be dependent on the matter of the brain. There is abundant evidence to show that the state of a person can alter the way internal parts of the body work.

Over a century ago a French physiologist called Claude Bernard worked with a soldier who had received a gunshot wound which had penetrated the stomach. The wound had never healed properly, and there was a permanent opening running between the inside of the soldier's stomach and the surface of his skin. This meant that Bernard could study the internal surface of the soldier's stomach while he deliberately altered the soldier's mood. To his surprise, he found that when he made the soldier angry, the lining blood vessels of his stomach flushed red with blood, and when he was calmed they blanched once again. A red face made a red stomach.

What we can learn from biofeedback and the alteration of *body* states by *mind* action, is that the *person-mind* can affect the body containing the mind in a real and measurable way. So when someone claims to be a healer and actually induces physical improvements in a sick person, then, using Occam's Razor, we need only to say that the sick person's mind was induced to change the state of his body by contact or rapport with the healer. The healer might simply be someone of strong character using nothing more paranormal than control by authoritarian demeanour to influence the patient.

The literature of psychosomatic illness – one held to be caused by mental stress – is full of accounts of patients who have developed often near lethal conditions as a result of acute mental stress, only to get better again when the stress was removed. We certainly cannot, at this stage of our enquiry, agree that someone who lays-on-hands to a sick person is necessarily doing something paranormal, although he may be.

I worked for a doctor who cured people by simply looking magnificent. He would sweep into the ward in a cloud of cologne, grey curls elegantly in place and leonine head inclined benignly. His manner would have put Donald Wolfit to shame. He dealt with ordinary mortals by attentive paternalism. I carried his case. He would stride into the ward leading a fawning retinue of mortal doctors and blushing nurses, like disciples from a biblical film epic. He would sit on the bed of the first patient, reaching forward to hold his wrist between manicured fingers then, for some seconds, he would stare meaningfully into their eyes remaining absolutely still. Finally, with a sense of timing he could have taught at drama school, he would intone with exquisitely measured mellifluence: 'You are much better.' Next day the patient would be much better. The doctor was an intolerant pig to work for and is now a knight.

I have no doubt at all that this particular doctor *did* cure people with the aid of practised melodrama, and the fact that he was a bit of a laughing stock among the common ruck of students does not diminish his healing ability. He did have it and he was also an intuitively accurate diagnostician. We ended up by respecting his clinical abilities and disliking only his Rolls-Royce.

I have also seen a group healing session which was more like a deep south revivalist meeting. There was singing, shouting and swaying and afterwards it was clear that every participant actually glowed with pleasure. Something important had happened to everyone there and it was only the reserved, Anglo-Saxon observer (myself) who had failed to gain anything from it, by trying to look in on it rather than to participate.

The knighted doctor would have entirely resisted any suggestion of paranormal abilities; I can imagine him turning puce at the mere suggestion. The leaders of the group session were redolent with psychological jargon and saw themselves as latter-day Freudian heroes. Two varieties of myth maker.

Two cardiologists discovered that the effect of morphine as a pain killer varied enormously from patient to patient. So they divided the patients into two groups, one was given morphine and the other a new drug they wanted to test. Thirty-eight per cent of the patients receiving the new drug were satisfactorily relieved of pain. The trouble was that the new drug was ordinary bicarbonate of soda which has no pain relieving properties at all as a drug, but clearly it does as a human conditioning agent. [1]

[1] Quoted in B. Inglis, *Natural Medicine*, Collins, London, 1979

This effect has been repeated literally hundreds of times and is known as the 'placebo effect'. I have seen it at work many times during my time as a medical doctor. A placebo is a 'dummy medicine' or, as the *Oxford Dictionary* puts it with some wryness, 'a medicine given to humour'. The placebo effect is to do with mythology; if the chalk pill or the bicarbonate of soda is presented as medicine, it is the power and superstition of the medical phalanx behind it which does the work of relief. A good proportion of medicine is to do with *reaction* to symptoms. I remember an old man with advanced cancer who was experiencing the most terrible pain which no drug would relieve. Finally, in desperation we carried out a leucotomy (an operation dividing fibres connecting the frontal part of the brain to the remainder). I spoke to him the day after the operation, asking how the pain was. He replied, 'It's exactly the same,' but he smiled as he said it. His *reaction* to the pain had changed altogether and so, in one sense, his pain *was* relieved.

As a 'highly qualified medical neurotic', I have suffered several 'lethal' diseases and each time it has taken a medical colleague some time and considerable patience to prove that my self-diagnosis was wrong.

So the mind-body-illness problem is very hard to crack, and the effect of people who call themselves healers is therefore difficult to assess. I am not suggesting at all that people who do call themselves healers are all working by suggestion, and perhaps deluding themselves and others that they do have special abilities. I am only suggesting that to find out whether these abilities are paranormal or not is very difficult indeed. At this stage we have to get as many pitfalls out of the way as possible. One way of approaching the problem might be to do a double-blind trial (see pages 36–7), but to equalise the personalities of 'healer' and 'dummy healer' is obviously impossible.

Another way is to look at the medical records of people who have been exposed to the laying-on of hands to see whether any objective clinical improvements were recorded. One study looked at 95 patients, most of whom had been treated by one healer. For 58 of them, it was impossible to get hold of the records. Of the remaining 37, in 22 cases the claims were at variance with the records; in 2 the healer contributed to the improvement of an organic condition; in 1 the organic disease was cured; in 3 it improved but relapsed; in 4 it improved but no change in organic state was recorded; in 4 the condition improved with orthodox treatment as well; and in 1 the patient failed to improve and deteriorated.

This strongly suggests that nothing much happened, but that would be far too hasty a judgement. The report was prepared by a medical doctor, and I am afraid we have to face the real problem of professional bias. When I was working as a doctor, one surgeon I worked for actually fiddled his results by special selection of cases; I came across many similar examples. Some members of the profession are firmly against healers simply because it threatens their authority base. It is a bit galling, after all, if you are treating a patient with all the modern technical methods without success, and along comes someone who simply touches the patient for him to get better. Fortunately, there is a rapidly increasing number of open-minded doctors who are entirely happy for healers to work with their patients, and a growing number of doctors occupying senior positions in orthodox medicine who are prepared to use alternative methods themselves.

Dr Peter Nixon is one of these enlightened people; he is senior consultant cardiologist at Charing Cross Hospital. For some time he has been treating cases of coronary thrombosis and other acute heart conditions with relaxation and meditation methods rather than by using intensive care alone. His results show that these alternative methods can be just as effective as the conventional treatment. He teaches his patients what he has termed the 'human function curve', which is a way of self-evaluating performance against stimulus. He is able to teach patients with high blood pressure how to lower their blood pressure, without drugs, from a thoroughly dangerous level to a figure which is entirely normal for age. [2]

[2] P. Nixon, The Practitioner, vol. 211, 1973; in O. Paul (ed.), Angina Pectoris, Medcom Press, New York; P. Nixon and H. J. Bethell, American Journal of Cardiology, vol. 33, 1974

This sort of treatment is not paranormal, and Dr Nixon would certainly not make any such claim. What his work *does* show is that these simpler patient–doctor relationships can be just as effective. For example, doctor–patient interaction of this sort has reached an extraordinary level in China. There is no doubt whatever that Chinese surgeons have performed open-chest surgery using only the insertion of tiny needles into the skin as anaesthesia. The effects of acupuncture are still under active debate, but there is no doubt that this did occur and that it was witnessed by more than one delegation of doctors from the British Medical Association.

If I said to a western patient, 'I'm going to take your appendix out and these two tiny needles in your ear lobe and your leg are all the anaesthetic you're going to get,' he would be out of the hospital in a flash. So what happens in China?

The physics we have been looking at so far shows that the best an experimenter can do is to look for *connections* and *interactions*, and so it follows that we cannot sit in an isolated, objective position, all that we can do is to see what happens between two systems. In this case, the two systems are healer and patient. The Chinese doctors describe it in what seems to me to be a very attractive way: 'The truth is communicated between unique pairs.' They here mean 'truth' to be the cure and the 'unique pair' being the rapport or special relationship which is set up between healer and patient.

But why was this not just hypnosis or autosuggestion? We have already seen how important suggestion is as a factor in the relief of symptoms. It was unlikely to have been hypnosis, because the patients were fully conscious during the whole of the operative procedure and were able to hold a normal conscious conversation with the nurses. The word 'suggestion' has no real meaning; it does not help in any way to explain *what* happened.

Hypnosis can relieve some physical conditions even, surprisingly, when they are genetically based. Hereditary congenital disorders are caused by genetic faults and it is hard to believe that they could be cured by hypnosis. Yet there is evidence that they have been relieved: congenital deformities of the skin, the blood vessels and the nails have all shown improvement. [3]

[3] S. Black, *Mind and Body*, William Kimber, London, 1969.

Perhaps the most useful comment we can make about acupuncture anaesthesia is that a very special connection is created between surgeon and patient, and this has much to do with the culture of China. It is particularly interesting in that respect that acupuncture is getting less common as a sole anaesthetic in China as the country becomes more westernised and industrialised. The culture of the Chinese is changing, and so their belief in the effectiveness of acupuncture becomes less. Their ideas of reality are changing.

We must ask therefore whether it is just a question of belief. I think *confidence* is perhaps a better word. Some doctors in this country in ordinary hospitals are encouraging their patients to develop enough confidence to alter their reactions of their own bodies, giving them 'permission to get better'. For example, Dr Alec Forbes was, until recently, Senior Medical Consultant at the Plymouth General Hospital. He frequently offered patients on the wards a choice of alternative therapies, with or without conventional hospital medicine. He also taught them to have confidence in their own choice and so to cure themselves. The successes he has achieved with alternative therapies do not need a paranormal assumption as an explanation.

What we have been looking at so far are the various ways in which patient, doctor, circumstance and culture can interact. If there were a paranormal effect in healing, we could assume either that the patient was altering the state of the *matter* of his body with his *mind*, or the healer was altering the matter of the patient's body with *his* mind. Or that the healer and the patient together were altering the *matter* of the patient's body with their combined minds. Or we could give up altogether and say that healing is a direct communication with God by means of prayer and meditation.

I do not at all want to belittle the belief that prayer is a very powerful healing influence; there are thousands of individual testimonies to its real curative value. What I want to do instead is look at experimental work which suggests that a healer can have an effect which is separable from the patient altogether. If that were shown to be the case, it would create the need for a paranormal explanation. It could be examined without having to assume a connection, rapport, or interaction between healer and patient. So now I want to look at people who claim to have healing powers which can exert a *direct* effect on the matter of another person or another living creature.

One of the people who has spent a lot of time investigating this possibility is Professor Bernard Grad of McGill University in Canada. Professor Grad works in the Department of Psychiatry at

Fig. 58
Professor Bernard Grad, experimental biologist at McGill University, who has studied the effects of healers on the growth of plants.

McGill University in Montreal and some time ago, he carried out a large number of experiments with someone who claimed to be able to heal both people and animals, a Hungarian called Oskar Estebany.

Estebany served in the Hungarian Cavalry and found that sick horses seemed to get better more quickly when he massaged them. Then he found the same was true when he applied his hands to sick people. But this sort of healing was officially frowned upon in his country and so he emigrated to Canada.

Professor Grad began experiments with Estebany and animals to try and discover whether what Estebany claimed to be able to do

was just a special relationship between healer and patient or
healer and animal, or whether a paranormal influence was at
work.

The experiments he did involved making small skin wounds on
anaesthetised mice. He traced the outline of each wound onto a
piece of transparent plastic to measure its area. The mice were
then divided into two groups and Estebany tried to heal one group
by the laying-on of hands. The other group was kept entirely
separate. The wounds in the group treated by him healed more
rapidly than the untreated group as measured by the reduction in
area of the wounds.

However, there are clearly a number of questions to be asked
here. Wounds in individual mice do not heal at an even rate. There
is a considerable variation. This was allowed for by comparing the
two groups as a whole and measuring averages. There is also the
'gentling' effect. If you stroke, and generally be rather nice to, one
half of a litter of animals, that half will probably grow more
rapidly and to a larger size than the other half. Although Estebany
had not touched the animals during the experiments and the
'gentling' effect was probably not important, Dr Grad did another
series of tests and divided the animals into three groups to
make doubly sure. The cages of all three groups were put inside
paper bags so that Estebany's contact with the animals was more
remote.

One group was exposed to the laying on of hands by Estebany. A
second group was exposed to a laying-on of hands by a group of
medical students who claimed no healing ability, and the third
group was not exposed to any influence at all. The animal technicians looking after all three groups were kept 'blind' as to which
group of animals were which, again to avoid a 'gentling' effect.
What Dr Grad found was that the group exposed to Estebany
healed more rapidly than the other two groups, and that the group
exposed to the non-healing of the medical students healed at the
same rate as the group exposed to nothing at all. This suggests that
an *interaction* or *connection* or *exchange of information* had
occurred between Estebany and the animals. The interaction was
unlikely to have been a rapport in the sense of a healer–patient
interaction. On balance it is likely that this was a paranormal
effect. The findings were small, but the experiments were well
designed. Dr Grad is very modest in his claims for experiments
involving some three hundred mice. I asked him about them:

KP: Dr Grad, one of the problems about healing is whether the
effect lies between two people, healer and patient, or whether

something else is involved that you might perhaps call 'para-normal', in the healer himself. Your experiments seem to show an effect from the healer.

BG: My experimental design was exactly the same as if instead of testing a healer I had tested a drug or a vitamin. We had large numbers of animals, we had several groups controlled, and we produced wounds of very definite size which we could measure. We did statistical analysis on the data and so in short, we did everything in a perfectly conventional way. The only thing that was different was to bring in a rather unusual type of treatment: the placing of the animal between the hands of a man who claimed to be able to heal. And I found on repeated experimentation that he could accelerate wound healing in a statistically reliable manner.

KP: One of the obvious criticisms made at the time was that in some way the treated animals were being 'gentled'.

BG: Yes, but the criticism is not valid because the gentling was done to all the animals including the controls prior to the separation of the groups and treatments, so it is not due to gentling. I am not saying that gentling cannot produce that effect, but the controls in this experiment were also gentled, so that we had no notion, when we were gentling, which animals were experimental and which controls.

KP: How do you view the results?

BG: What Estebany really showed me was that he could accelerate wound healing in mice under double-blind conditions, and that results shown by statistical analysis could not be due to chance. This to me was mind boggling – the fact that the simple act of holding animals between the hands could accelerate a process such as healing.

KP: And you felt there was something going from the healer to the animals?

BG: I could think of no other explanation. One of the other controls we used was heat, and this by itself did not have any effect either, so it must have been something else. I couldn't think of anything coming from the sweat of the hands which would accelerate healing. Estebany kept on talking about an energy, and in the course of further experiments my inclination was to believe that this is so. I'm inclined to feel that there is an energy, whatever its nature, that is active.

There will always remain a doubt that there could have been some normal person–animal interaction, some physiological interplay which Dr Grad did not control for. So he continued work with Estebany; the next time with barley seeds. What he did was to grow barley seeds under evenly controlled conditions and exposes one half to the laying-on of hands by Estebany, and leaving the other half unexposed.

Barley seeds grow up like blades of grass, and their number and height can be measured. Estebany performed laying-on of hands on one group of barley seedlings and also on the solution used to water them. Dr Grad's idea was to 'ill-treat' the barley seedlings, to keep them under-watered and over-salted, so he watered them with a dilute salt solution to keep them in need. What he found was that the seeds treated by the healer showed a higher yield than the untreated. They were, on average, taller and more numerous.

The obvious objection is that there must be a large and normal variation in the growth of barley seeds. There is, so he repeated the whole experiment, but Estebany was allowed to have nothing to do with either group of seeds. Grad found that there was no statistical difference between the two, so he could reasonably claim that Estebany affected the growth of barley seeds by the laying-on of hands. In further experiments, Dr Grad eventually found that Estebany could affect the growth of the seedlings by laying-on of hands to the bottle of the solution alone. Whatever he did appeared to work through the solution he watered them with.

Dr Grad's experiments are of good design and careful statistical analysis and show that there is a small but definite effect which comes from the healer and is not to do with healer–patient rapport, cultural influence or other human–human interaction. I asked Dr Grad what conclusion he drew from these experiments.

BG: The thing what's especially remarkable to me about the barley seed experiments is that Estebany did not have to come in contact with the seeds directly. We found that it was possible just to stimulate barley seed growth by pouring on water which had been held in his hand. He had to hold it not for a few seconds, but for half an hour, and there may well be a dose–response relationship here between the length of time that you hold the water in the hand and the kind of effect that was shown. Something must have passed from his hand to the solution which was then delivered to the seeds. And since the treatment in most of the experiments was through the barrier of a sealed glass container, it cannot be a material substance in the sense that it is a chemical of any kind.

I know of no other way to explain these experiments, and so I'm inclined to feel that there was something from the hand that was being radiated and this penetrated the glass bottle and went in and altered the water. There's some evidence now that properties of water themselves are changed by this process. This is some evidence; I published some of it, others have done more.

KP: Is this something to do with the analysis of the water, the constitution of water?

BG: It has to do with the hydrogen bonding. There is no change in the chemical composition of the water.

KP: It's still H_2O.

BG: It's still H_2O, but it's just that the way in which the molecules are linked up to each other which is changed.

KP: Do you regard Estebany's influence as paranormal?

BG: People call it paranormal, but in my view it's no more paranormal than magnetism was paranormal five hundred years ago. It's simply that we have not paid any attention to this kind of phenomenon, and so we did not investigate what the nature of the energy is.

I don't feel that I'm functioning as a parapsychologist in this at all; I feel that I'm functioning as a normal conventional biologist investigating something that is poorly understood simply because it has not been investigated. It's something that's been around for thousands of years. I call it the best-kept secret of the millennium; that people have the ability to influence biological processes whether in other people or in other organisms, or even in matter.

KP: Why do you think it's such a 'well-kept secret', as you put it?

[4] B. Grad, *Journal of American Society for Psychical Research*, vol. 59, 1965; with R. Cadaret and G. Paul, *International Journal of Parapsychology*, vol. 3, 1961; vol. 5, 1963; vol. 6, 1964; *Journal of American Society for Psychical Research*, vol. 61, 1967

BG: There are some people, I'm afraid, who are so constituted that the whole notion of this frightens them. They have set their minds on another type of paradigm[pattern of rules] of reality and this shakes that paradigm.

Professor Grad has published several accounts of his work. [4]

Dr Justa Smith is a biochemist and works in Buffalo. She is also a member of a religious order and she heard about Dr Grad's work and wrote:

Although Dr Grad's data were convincing, I maintain my scepticism towards the possibility of a paranormal healer effecting a true cure. However, I did obtain his services [Estebany, the healer who worked with Dr Grad] ... and hypothesised that the healing force channelled through and activated by the hands of this paranormal healer must affect the activity of an enzyme in order that healing could possibly take place. [Enzymes are biological catalysts which assist body chemistry to work without taking part in the actual chemistry.]

Dr Sister Justa Smith, to give her her full title, then subjected Estebany to a long series of tests to find out whether he could alter the level of activity of an enzyme by laying-on of hands to a bottle of the enzyme. He could and did, so we must conclude that the biochemistry of a complex protein in a bottle was changed by an influence brought to bear on it by a healer. Since, like Dr Grad, Dr Justa Smith carried out the necessary control measures, I am bound to conclude that a paranormal influence was at work here. Like Dr Grad, Dr Justa Smith has published her findings. [5]

Two other investigators did the following experiments. They anaesthetised a group of mice with the same dose of anaesthetic and then try and awaken them. The mice that the subject concentrated on awoke on average sooner than the control group, at odds against chance of 100,000 to 1. [6] And this work has now been repeated. [7] From the experiment it is reasonable to conclude that someone who says he can heal can indeed bring a paranormal influence to bear on living matter.

I am bound to confess here that of all the aspects of the paranormal I have written about, healing is the one I had most personal trouble with. This is entirely due to the irrational prejudices and biases implanted in my mind during my training as a doctor. There is still a part of my head that is trying to dismiss the whole thing as a human indulgence. Another part of my head is convinced by a considerable volume of well designed and conducted experimentation.

Matters are changing for the better. More and more doctors are willing to admit healers into hospital wards to help the sick, and since I am aware of the medical prejudices still resonating in my own head, this is an optimistic step forward and one which minimises the danger of going to a healer with what might turn out to be an acutely dangerous condition that could be put right with a known and orthodox medical procedure.

Paranormal healing is yet another example of connection and

[5] J. M. Smith, *The Dimensions of Healing*, Academy of Parapsychology and Medicine, 1972

[6] G. and A. Watkins, *Journal of Parapsychology*, vol. 35, 1971

[7] R. Wells and J. Klein, *Journal of Parapsychology*, vol. 36, 1972

interaction. I have tried to show that the new physics is also mainly concerned with connection and interactions and so I want to look now at some of the most recent work in physics which is beginning to show truly astonishing and unusual connections between what appear to be entirely separate parts of the universe.

13. The Whole is Greater than the Parts

Current physics has progressed beyond the idea that there is an outside world lying somewhere entirely separate from ourselves. It has shown very clearly instead that there are real and functional connections between our minds and the world around us and that our human senses do not and cannot appreciate this more variable world of space-time, interaction and exchange as an objective and real place.

To see how it is that paranormal events like remote viewing, telepathy, metal bending and paranormal healing might work, I want in this chapter to look at some really very new physics, which suggests that there may be an entire part of the universe hidden away, not only from our senses but from most of our measuring instruments as well. Also that in this world of shadows may lie the beginnings of an explanation for what we now call the paranormal.

The story of this unexpected development in physics begins with a famous 'thought experiment'. A 'thought experiment' is carried out on paper usually by a group of scientists who have a problem they want to solve, but have neither the money, the apparatus nor the time available actually to perform the experiment. A thought experiment usually begins by someone saying, 'What would happen if....?', and the difference between what then follows and the creation of science fiction is that the game is played absolutely for real and there are no logical holds barred. Reason, correlation and refutation are followed to the limit.

In 1935 three physicists published their analysis of a thought experiment.[1] Their names were Albert Einstein, Boris Podolsky and Nathan Rosen. Physicists know the experiment as the 'Einstein–Podolsky–Rosen paradox' and usually talk about it as the 'EPR paradox' or the 'EPR effect'. It has been called 'The Pandora's Box of Modern Physics'. [2]

There is no question at all that the EPR effect and the physics which has followed from it is very strange and requires a severe re-adjustment of the head to get a firm, conceptual grasp of the

[1] A. Einstein, B. Podolsky and N. Rosen, *Physical Review*, vol. 47, 1935

[2] G. Zukav, *The Dancing Wu Li Masters*, Rider Hutchinson, London, 1979

basic idea. It is actually very simple, but this basic idea is *so shocking* that my first reaction having read it was to go and hide my head in the sand muttering: 'All the world is mad except thee and me and even thee is a little odd.' Niels Bohr wrote: 'Anyone who is not shocked by quantum theory has not understood it.'

To get a grip on this strange concept I am going to begin with two guns (Fig. 59) pointing in two exactly opposite directions. I then arrange for some electronics to fire the guns at exactly the same time (ignoring relativity). The bullets fly away in opposite directions and after a definite time, say one hundredth of a second, the bullets pass two points in their path where their speed is measured.

Figs. 59–62. A large-scale analogy for the EPR experiments.

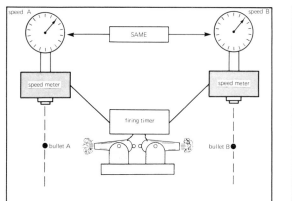 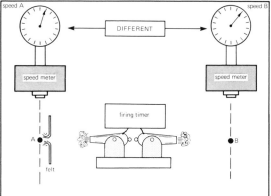

Fig. 59
Two similar bullets fired from similar guns will achieve the same speed. Nothing done to bullet *A* will affect bullet *B* after they have left their respective guns. Bullets *A* and *B* are not correlated.

Fig. 60
Here bullet *A* will be recorded as travelling slower than *B*, because it has had to penetrate the felt. But again, nothing done to either bullet will affect the other.

Assuming that the same amount of explosive had been packed into each cartridge and that barrel diameters and bullet weights were all much the same, I have every reason to expect that the speed of each bullet will also be recorded as much the same.

I now repeat the experiment, but this time (Fig. 60) I make one difference. I put a piece of felt in the way of one bullet (*A*) just before it passes by the speed measuring device. I fire the guns simultaneously again, bullet *B* reaches its speed measurer and bullet *A* reaches its speed measurer having blasted its way through the felt.

Because *A* has passed through the felt, some of its kinetic energy (energy resulting from motion) will have been dissipated; it will be slightly slowed down and so the speed measuring device will read its speed as slower than bullet *B*. Bullet *B* achieves tolerably the same speed as *A* and *B* in the first experiment without the felt.

The point about this simple arrangement is that nothing I do to bullet *A* while it is in flight will affect bullet *B* while it is in flight.

Using a word I defined earlier on, once the two bullets are in flight, there are no *correlations* between them; they behave totally independently. Only things happening in their own vicinity will affect their speed or path. If I put (Fig. 61) a piece of steel obliquely in the path of bullet *A*, take away the felt and fire the guns, then

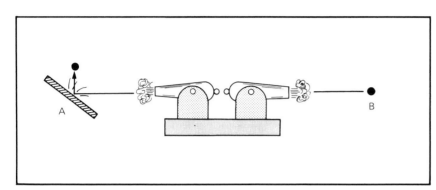

Fig. 61
If bullet *A* ricochets off a metal plate, bullet *A* will change direction, but cannot affect bullet *B*'s direction.

bullet *A* will ricochet off the steel and its path direction will change. This again will have no effect on the path of bullet *B*. Once more there is no *correlation* between the path of the two bullets; they are again behaving independently.

This independence in the sub-atomic world of physics is called 'the principle of local causes' and says exactly the same thing: that events in two places behave as if there is no connection or correlation between either event or place. This is an entirely reasonable conclusion, or at least, so it seems.

Einstein, Podolsky and Rosen were worrying about a part of physics called quantum theory (the part of physics which deals with energy and radiation as if both were composed of elementary packets or *quanta*) which others like Bohr and Heisenberg were regarding as a complete theory. The EPR trio were trying to show that quantum theory was *not* complete, but what others read into their EPR paradox was quite different and led directly, much to the chagrin of the trio, to the idea that the principle of local causes can fail: in an experiment rather similar to the bullets, one bullet could affect the other *after* they had both left their respective barrels.

Obviously if the two bullets were fired so their paths crossed (Fig. 62) the shock wave from one could affect the path and velocity of the other. But fired in exactly opposite directions there is just no way in which one can affect the other. So all our common sense demands that in the case of the bullets, the principle of local causes succeeds, or that one bullet can only be affected by events around it.

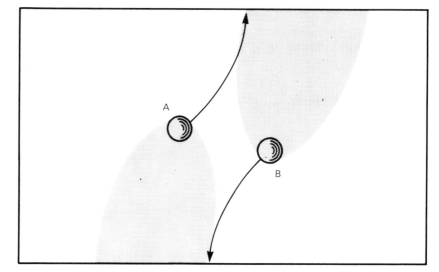

Fig. 62
Only if bullets *A* and *B* are allowed to pass sufficiently close to each other for their shock waves to interfere could one bullet affect the other after both have left the guns. The principle of local causes holds.

Figs. 63– 6. *How 'interference' experiments carried out with single photons show the breakdown of the principle of local causes.*

Now consider some very small bullets, particles (quanta) of light, called photons. A photon is, strictly speaking, the unit of electromagnetic radiation. Light can be looked at as electromagnetic radiation, so we can speak of a photon of light as a unit of light. In 1801 an English physicist called Thomas Young arranged a very simple experiment (Fig. 63). He put an opaque screen with two parallel slits in it between a source of light and a screen. The slits were narrow and could be either open or closed. When he opened one slit, a patch of light appeared on the screen;

Fig. 63
Thomas Young's classic experiment of 1801 demonstrated the wave nature of light by showing that two beams interfered with each other. In Fig. 63, a screen with two narrow slits in it is put between a light and a screen. Each slit can be open or closed. If one slit is opened, an even patch of light is seen on the screen.

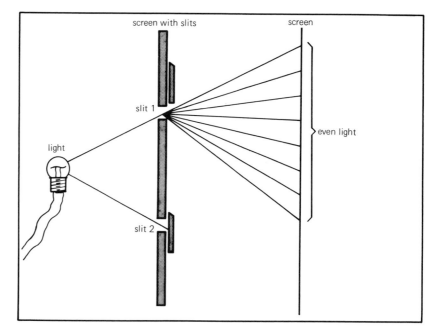

there was a bit of spread of the light due to another feature of light, diffraction, but the screen was evenly lit.

When Thomas Young opened both slits (Fig. 64), he might have expected to see two even patches of light, one from each slit, perhaps overlapping a bit in the middle. What he actually saw was

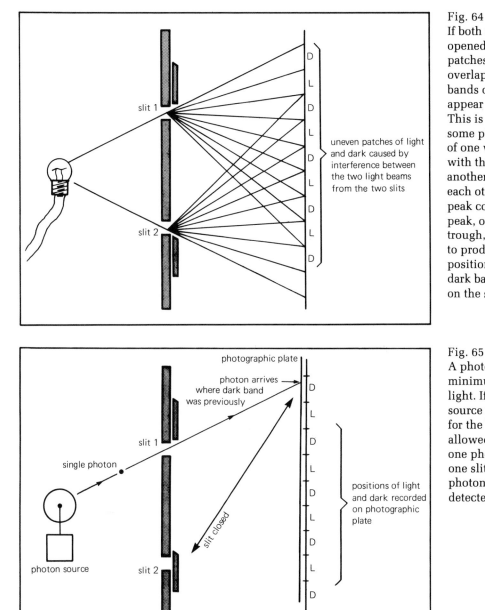

Fig. 64
If both slits are opened, the two patches of light overlap, and alternate bands of light and dark appear on the screen. This is because in some places the peaks of one wave coincide with the troughs of another, and cancel each other out. Where peak coincides with peak, or trough with trough, the waves add to produce light. The position of light and dark bands are marked on the screen.

Fig. 65
A photon is a minimum packet of light. If a photon source is substituted for the bulb and allowed to release just one photon, and just one slit is open, the photon will be detected at the screen.

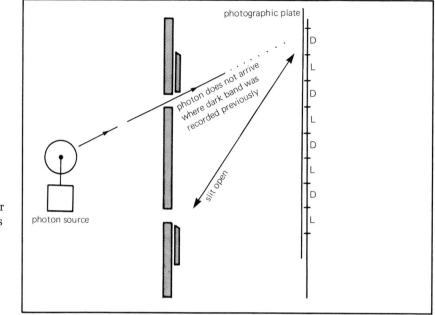

Fig. 66
If the experiment is repeated with the other slit open, the photon is not detected in the position of a dark band. It does not arrive. How did it 'know' that the other slit was open?

a pattern of light and dark bands. The light from one slit had in some way interacted with the light from the other slit. This interaction, called 'interference' because one beam of light interferes with another, can easily be explained by assuming the wave-like behaviour of light. The waves of light from one slit arrive in the 'up' part of the wave motion and the waves of light from the other slit arrive at the same place in the 'down' part of the wave motion and so cancel each other out producing a patch of non-light or darkness.

We now photograph the screen with both slits open and mark on the screen where the *light* patches are and where the *dark* patches are. We now re-work the experiment, this time using a light source which emits such a small amount of light that it can fire just one photon of light, or one fundamental unit of light (Fig. 65).

We do the experiment with one slit open and use a very sensitive photographic plate on the screen to record the impact of the photon. We record it successfully, but note that it hit in a place which would have been dark if both slits had been open. We then fire another photon in exactly the same direction *but* now with the second slit open. The photon does not arrive. There is only darkness on the photographic plate.

In other words, the single photon behaves as though it was interfering with light from the other slit, so producing darkness.

But there *was no light* from the other slit, and the photon could not interfere with itself.

The awe-inspiring question which physicists have been asking ever since is: How did the photon know the other slit was open? 'Know' is the mind-boggling word in that question. If it 'knew', what was the information it reacted to?

A single particle with the principle of local causes only affecting its behaviour actually behaves as if it is reacting to information from somewhere else which is non-local. (It is not strictly correct to talk of single particles. I have deliberately simplified this experiment. Photons are actually measured statistically and not as units, but the basic reasoning still remains true.) What is worse, the change in behaviour is almost instantaneous; that is to say, in space-time it has to be *faster* than light because it is *affecting* light, or it has to be outside space-time.

One might use complementarity as a way of avoiding this awful problem, and say that this proves that to look at light as a stream of photons or particles was just a mistake and if only we had kept to the idea of waves we would not have had this problem. However, there is excellent evidence – the photo-electric effect – for the existence of photons and they are not a mistake and so we are left with the thoroughly uneasy idea that a photon 'knows' something, or is informed in an apparently impossible way about an event somewhere else – non-locally.

Now let us return to the two guns and the EPR paradox: the two bullets show no interaction or correlation when one of them is affected during its flight; the principle of local causes works. Instead of the two guns, imagine (Fig. 67) a machine which can emit elementary particles of matter in exactly opposite directions, and imagine also that only single particles are flying in opposite directions away from the machine. (Again, I have described this work as if single particles were involved, when in fact the presence of particles are measured statistically – that is to say, it is the probability of arrival which is calculated.)

The machine can be contrived so that any two particles, one going in one direction and the other going in an exactly opposite direction, are given exactly opposite properties. One of the properties which elementary particles can be given by a machine is *spin*. Rather like a ball from a cricket bowler, they can be given a clockwise spin or an anti-clockwise spin – one particle has a 'leg-break' and another an 'off-break'. Some particles have no spin at all.

The machine can also be adjusted so that it will accept a stream of particles (Fig. 67) with a random spin (leg-break and off-break

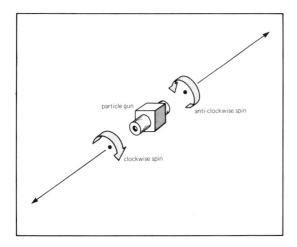 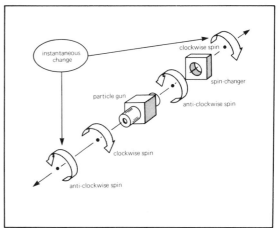

Fig. 67
A particle gun, like the bullet-firing guns, can be arranged to emit two streams of particles in opposite directions. Like a cricket ball, the particles can be given clockwise or anti-clockwise spins.

Fig. 68
If a special magnet is placed in the path of the anti-clockwise spinning stream, it instantly changes the direction of the spin to clockwise. As this happens, the opposite, clockwise-spin, stream *also* changes its spin direction, instantaneously. The bullets from the gun could not affect one another after they had left the barrels of the gun, but here one stream of particles can affect the other stream.

particles), and split them up into two streams, one with a clockwise spin and another with an anti-clockwise spin. It can also be arranged so that this effect is completely even in both beams. This means that if we measure the spin in one stream, we know that the spin in the other stream is exactly opposite, because that is what the machine was designed to do to the particles.

Suppose that the machine has settled down and both streams are spinning stably in opposite directions (Fig. 68). We then reverse the spin in one stream with another machine. We find a really shocking result: the spin in the other stream reverses instantaneously. Since both particle streams are travelling at effectively the speed of light, very few interpretations of this highly uncomfortable result are possible. There are basically three possible answers:

1 *The whole of modern physics is wrong.* There is very little evidence to support such an assumption.
2 *Information gets around the universe faster than light.* Physicists are resisting this conclusion because the velocity of light is fundamental to so many other areas of physics.
3 *Things which appear to be separate are not.* They are in fact *connected* in some unobserved way.

In conversation with physicists I have found that the third answer is the most favoured at the present. What this means is that the principle of local causes fails, because a change in one beam at a point distant to the other affects the other instantaneously. Put in the way of physicists: there is a *correlation* between the two beams. This, very simply stated, is the basis of the Einstein–Podolsky–Rosen paradox.

The experiment was formulated by Einstein to prove the incompleteness of quantum theory, but much later he wrote about it and said something extraordinary: 'One can escape from this conclusion only by assuming that measuring S_1 (that is one particle stream) *telepathically* [sic] changes the real situations of S_2 (the other particle stream) or by denying independently real situation as such to things which are spatially separated from each other.' [3]

When the EPR trio published their thought experiment, it remained just that. It was not until quite recently that the EPR experiment was actually performed, and an operational connection was established between events and structures which should have no connection at all. [4]

At the time of writing about six different groups have also carried out similar experiments on the EPR paradox; broadly speaking they confirm the basic conclusion: things and events which should have no connection at all and which are separate in space do show a connection, and therefore the principle of local causes continues to show serious faults.

The paranormal and physics now seem to be moving closer together. I would now like to look again at the Ganzfeld and remote viewing experiments.

Both sender and receiver in Ganzfeld, and outbound and inbound subjects in remote viewing should, by the old physics, show no connection or correlation at all. Yet the evidence from experiment shows that there is a connection and there are correlations. This seems to me an important similarity, and I will return to it later.

The basic language of physics is mathematics, which has no place in a general book like this. Physicists prefer where possible to have a taut mathematical structure from which to argue, and in 1964 a physicist at the CERN establishment in Switzerland, Dr J. S. Bell, published an entirely mathematical paper which has since become known as 'Bell's theorem'.

The conclusion of this pioneering mathematical analysis, in language terms, was this: either quantum physics is fundamentally wrong or the principle of local causes fails. From a purely theoretical point of view, Dr Bell had arrived at a similar conclusion to the physicists who had experimented on the EPR paradox: that there had to be connections and correlations between events and structures which were spatially separate.

However, the difference between the EPR paradox and Bell's theorem is that the EPR paradox deals with sub-atomic particles like photons, whereas Bell's theorem covers large (macroscopic)

[3] A. Einstein, *Autobiographical Notes*, Harper and Row, New York, 1949

[4] S. Freedman and J. Clauser, *Physical Review Letters*, vol. 28, 1972

[5] H. Stapp, *Physical Review*, vol. 3, 1977

[6] H. Stapp, *Bell's Theorem and World Process*, Il Nuovo Cimento, vol. 29, 1975

everyday objects like tables and skyscrapers. As physicist Professor Henry Stapp has written: 'The important thing about Bell's theorum is that it puts the dilemma posed by quantum phenomena clearly into the realm of macroscopic phenomena.' [5] Many physicists I have spoken to regard Bell's theorem as the most significant advance in physics since the early part of the century. Again, Stapp wrote: 'Bell's theorem is the most profound discovery of science.' [6] Its importance lies in the fact that by entirely rigorous mathematics it has shown that our most clearly held views about the way the universe is put together and works are profoundly and fundamentally wrong. What this physics is now clearly leading towards, in both theory and experiment, is that: the universe as a mass of separate parts and energies is slowly being replaced by a view which says that there is a fundamental unity and inseparability.

In such a universe, the paranormal becomes entirely possible, because if physicists are saying that information can be exchanged between objects with no measurable connection, which are separate in space – as happens in the EPR effect – then there is no reason at all why information should not also be exchanged between human beings who are separate in space and who also have no measurable connection.

Experience tells us that human beings miles apart are affected only by events around them, or – put in terms of physics – that they exhibit no correlation in their behaviour, and the principle of local causes holds. Experiments on the paranormal, however, show that there *can* be correlations and connections between human beings miles apart and that the principle of local causes, too, probably fails.

This seems to me the crux of any comparison between current physics and the paranormal. It is premature to say that this very new physics of local causes, the EPR paradox and Bell's theorem, *explain* the paranormal, but it does, in my view, provide an increasingly firm intellectual framework which is likely to explain it in the future.

The EPR paradox, the experiments which have stemmed from it, and Bell's theorem, are leading a gradually increasing number of scientists into a physics where the ordinary sequences of analysis and research are reversed.

In conversation, David Bohm uses language with a very special care. He is astoundingly quick at picking up a lapse in syntax or the sloppy use of words. But he is not an etymologist; he is Professor of Physics in Birkbeck College at the University of London. As I write he has just published a remarkable book called

Wholeness and the Implicate Order,[7] in which he describes his world-view which is a result of a lifetime of experimental and theoretical work in physics. Like all people who think in an original direction, he takes time to expand on his views, since he wants very clearly to establish that his listener has found a rapport with his way of explaining things, and that he is not wasting time.

In his book, he writes of a physics which begins with a reversed assumption. Earlier (see page 11), I described the difference between a 'holist' and a 'reductionist'; a reductionist is a scientist who dissects and breaks up the universe into smaller and smaller pieces and hopes to be able to understand the whole by re-assembling all the pieces. David Bohm's physics is the reverse of this; he starts with the assumption of an unbroken whole universe: 'We must turn physics around. Instead of starting with parts and showing how they work together, we start with the whole.'[8]

David Bohm's view is that at the most profound level of the universe everything – space, time, matter and energy – are all unified into a single universal unity, and it is only we, from our human, sensory position, who see things as the separate pieces of space, time and matter.

This part of nature, the unity, he calls the 'implicate' or enfolded universe, and the parts that we are aware of he calls the 'explicate' or unfolded universe. David Bohm uses explicate and implicate in their etymological sense as derived from *plicare* (to fold). He develops the view, for example, that an electron or a shower of electrons are constantly popping up into explicate order from the ground base of the implicate order in a kind of permanent cosmic dance between actual electron-like existence, and non-existence: manifest electrons and non-manifest electrons.

It is worthwhile pointing out again that David Bohm has not come to this view of things out of a philosophical creative need alone, but because it solves more problems and explains more unknowns in the more rigorous world of mathematical physics, than do more 'traditional' approaches.

To give his idea visual shape, he has created two visual thought forms, one of which he made, and the other which we created in the television studio from a drawing in his book.

The first (Fig. 69) is a cylindrical jar full of glycerine. In the centre of the jar there is a rod which can be rotated. With an ink dropper, we put one drop of black ink on the top surface of the glycerine. It does not sink in, but remains where it is because the glycerine is viscous or sticky.

We now rotate the centre rod once and the ink drop is first

[7] D. Bohm, *Wholeness and The Implicate Order*, Routledge and Kegan Paul, London, 1980

[8] Quoted in G. Zukav, *The Dancing Wu Li Masters* (op. cit.), from a lecture delivered by Bohm at Berkeley, University of California

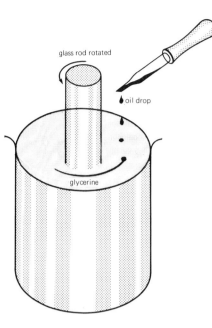

Fig. 69
David Bohm's analogy for his 'implicate universe': a jar of glycerine with a glass rod in it. The rod can be rotated. A blob of ink is dropped onto the glycerine. When the rod is rotated through, say, one full revolution, the ink blob thins out and disappears as the glycerine shears. When the rod is rotated through a full revolution in the opposite direction, the ink blob gradually reassembles. This example is used by Professor Bohm to explain how elementary particles could 'project' into reality (the assembled blob) from an implicate or 'enfolded' reality (the disassembled blob).

drawn out into a thin line and then disappears altogether. We put a second drop on top of the glycerine and turn the rod once more; that drop too draws out into a thin line and disappears. Then we add a third drop, and so on.

Three electrons (ink drops) have become enfolded into the implicate universe. Three electron-like things have become non-electrons. Three manifest electrons have become non-manifest.

Now we reverse the rotation of the rod (this is really spectacular to watch): the third ink drop beings to reappear, first as a line which gets thicker, and then reassembled into a drop. We give the rod another turn and the second drop begins to reappear in the same way, but now the third drop begins to disappear in the opposite direction. Finally we give the rod another turn, and the first ink drop reappears, whilst the second drop begins to disappear. The model does not suggest that the drops are moving forwards or backwards in time, but rather into and out of the implicate universe – or manifesting and unmanifesting.

Two crucial points about David Bohm's physics emerge from this simple visual analogy. First, that matter appears and disappears between the enfolded or implicate orders, and secondly that we know something about where it goes when it disappears.

If we imagine the glycerine jar to be the whole universe, we can write down the relation between action and objects in that universe. We know that the disappearance and reappearance of one ink drop (one electron or elementary particle) is related to one turn of the rod, so we could write that one turn clockwise creates one electron in the explicate order, or that one turn anticlockwise removes one electron to the enfolded implicate order.

How does all this square up with the consistent, static, hard-edged universe of day-to-day activity? In David Bohm's universe, matter is constantly manifesting and unmanifesting between explicate and implicate universes, but there is a temporary and consistent condition which is the everyday world. It is as if matter is in a constant froth of manifestation and unmanifestation but, rather like a ciné film racing through the gate of a projector, our everyday universe is stationary on the screen as a stable picture of real life; and this is what we perceive as our sensory reality. In fact he *calls* the matter of our everyday sensory reality *a projection*. He uses two television cameras and a fish tank to illustrate the idea (Fig. 70).

Fig. 70
Another of David Bohm's analogies, taken from his book *Wholeness and the Implicate Order*. [7] A fish in a tank is viewed by two cameras. One shows it head-on, the other side-on. If an observer is able to look *only* at the two screens, and knows nothing about television, then, as the fish moves, the two images are seen to be correlated. Professor Bohm uses this idea to illustrate the idea that what we perceive as everyday reality (the two screens) is a series of projections from an enfolded or implicate part of the universe where things are not manifest. We find connections between our various images of the world around us, which are related to and perhaps produced by another aspect of nature, which is perhaps unavailable either to our senses or to our instruments. It is perhaps by this means that the connections of paranormal events may occur.

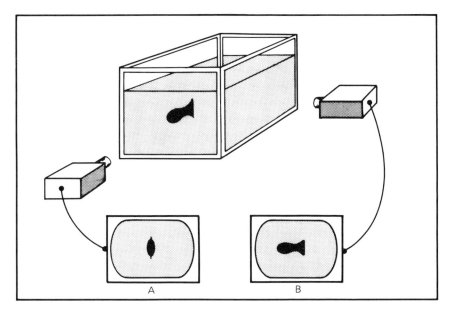

The two cameras at right angles to each other are both recording an image of the fish, and the two screens show two different pictures: one of the fish head-on and the other of it side-on. There's nothing odd about that. It is no more than we expect, since everyone knows how television cameras work and in any case, we have the overview of our own senses looking at the whole apparatus to explain why we see two different images.

Now the fish changes its position. What do we then see on the two screens? Supposing the fish turns through a right angle. Then over a period of a few seconds, the image on one screen is gradually transformed into that which was on the other. If it then moves back to its previous position, there is a gradual transformation back to the previous views which were on the screens. Again, nothing remarkable about that.

Consider correlations and local causes again; we now see a correlation between the two pictures and of course, in everyday terms, the correlation is simply explained by the television apparatus. If we know nothing except what is on the two screens, and nothing about television, we see two objects spatially separate, but one *affects* the other and vice versa. The two spatially separate things are well and truly *correlated*, yet one does not cause the other. The content of one picture passes into the other and vice versa.

Now we can say something much more interesting: the content of one image manifests in the other without cause, and it is perfectly clear that it is not *local* causes in the screens that are affecting the two images. So we have to look somewhere else for an explanation of the correlations or connections between the two screens. David Bohm describes this model in his book [7]:

... the images on the two screens are two-dimensional projections (or facets) of a three-dimensional reality. In some sense this three-dimensional reality holds these two projections within it. Yet since these projections exist only as abstractions, the three-dimensional reality is neither of these, but rather it is something else, something of a nature beyond both.

For the television series, I talked to Professor Bohm about his view of the world as a physicist and how he saw paranormal metal bending:

DB: I have no opinion on that as at present, but assuming that it did take place, I could make some comments. We can think that thought in itself is information – and there's a neuro-physiologist called Pribram working in California who has got some reasonable evidence that memory, for example, is not stored in particular cells of the brain, but all over – holographically. It's folded into the whole brain and unfolds to make images of things that are localised. Now, you can say, 'How does the body move?' You may think you want to move from one place to another, but you cannot say how this thought gets you to move. There's a gap there, and when you move, the movement takes place from all over the brain and body in a way that you do not see. The thought, somehow, is a display of where you want to go and the whole nervous system is watching this display and somehow getting you together. So that flow, that display of information, organises flow all over the body and the nervous system, so as to get you to go from one place to another in ways that nobody could possibly describe.

KP: Supposing it was the case that the idea of metal bending was finally and fully validated in experimental terms; you seem to be providing a clear intellectual framework in which physics would not have any real problem?

DB: Yes. If you say that all matter actually works from information, even an electron is forming from empty space – being informed, as it were, by some unknown source of information which may be all over this space. [Information is a form of energy and energy is interchangeable with matter. So information is connected with matter.] And there's *no sharp division between thought, emotion and matter* [KP's italics]. They flow into each other, you see. Even in an ordinary experience, you form an emotion which flows into a movement of matter in the body, or the movement of matter in the body gives rise to emotion and thought. Science has no idea whatsoever how thought could directly affect an object which is not in contact with the body, but if you say that the entire ground of existence is enfolded in space, that all matter is coming out of that space – including ourselves, our brains, our thoughts and the thing you want to bend – then information might readily pervade the space so that matter itself starts to change. You could say matter is always forming according to whatever information it has, and therefore a thought process could alter that information content; I'd say that it does look possible, though I think very careful experiments have to be done before we say whether it actually does take place.

One new part of physics is therefore suggesting that matter and the universe itself may have connections and correlations in an enfolded universe where there seem to be no clear causes and effects, but only connections. No space-time, but only interactions. It seems that all the pieces of the universe, including ourselves, are manifesting and unmanifesting in a constant dynamism. We, too, are made of the same atoms and particles of the universe, and experiments on the paranormal are also showing that there are connections and interactions between apparently separate people.

It looks as if we can look at the universe around us in many totally different ways. Like the complementarity of Niels Bohr and the other great innovating physicists of his era, it may be that these different ways are not at all mutually exclusive but are another example of the multiple interactions of the human mind. Each description is just one facet of the entire interaction between ourselves and the universe, just as one physicist will design an experiment to show light to be a wave motion, and another will design an experiment to show light to be a stream of particles, and *both* are correct. It may be that the view of reality assumed by an investigator of the paranormal may actually depict the results he gets.

In the last chapter I want to summarise what we have been examining so far, then to ask the scientists who took part in our series to speculate on how they see the future of physics and the paranormal.

14. Ways of Knowing

If there are functional interactions between things which are separate in space and time and to our senses, and if research into the paranormal reveals similar interactions between human minds which are also separate in space, then we are bound to review the way we know things, because the ordinary, everyday view of the world does not include such notions and so cannot be complete.

To try and weld these two views together, I am going to extend the basic idea of complementarity in this last chapter to cover the different ways in which we do get to know about the world inside and outside our minds.

Earlier, I was looking at 'dualists' and 'monists'. The dualist holds the view that his mind and perceptions are separate from the world he observes, and the monist holds the view that there is a fundamental unity of mind and universe and any thoughts to the contrary are purely illusory. For this reason: most dualists are reductionists and most monists are holists.

The complementarity of physics gave us one very important way of understanding viewpoints like this which are otherwise mutually exclusive. Just as it is possible to consider light as a wave motion *and* a stream of particles simultaneously, so is it possible to accept the view of the world our senses tell us about *and* the view of the world which proposes that everything is in some way connected together by strands which lie outside the realm of our senses and everyday experience.

In the first view, the world of the senses, minds communicating paranormally and minds affecting matter are concepts which are absolutely impossible. In the world of universal connection and interaction, there is no problem at all in accepting both these ideas, since interaction between things which are already connected poses no logical problem.

So far, I have made it look as if an experiment is the only way to test whether something is true or not. But this is not the whole answer. I pick up a biscuit and put it in my mouth. I know perfectly well that biscuit will get to my mouth, without experiment.

If I am miserable because I have a pain in the stomach, I do not need anyone experimenting with my pain responses or my stomach. I *have* a pain in the stomach and no external scientist is ever going to convince me that the pain was not a real pain or that the pain was not severe. I *know*, *experience* and can modify the pain, and that is my own reality.

Now I want to return to a strange conclusion of some work I referred to earlier (see page 28). Lawrence Le Shan's experiment with the different descriptions of the universe showed that when key words like 'relativity' and 'Brahma' were taken out, no one could distinguish whether a particular description was written by a mystic or a physicist. [1] The descriptions were entirely similar in meaning and content. However, one other feature of this experiment is quite shocking and needs explanation.

Many of the descriptions of the universe by the mystics were made more than a thousand years ago, before the age of reason, centuries before the construction of the giant atomic accelerators, and without any of the mathematics which form the basis of current physics. So it is entirely reasonable to ask: how is it that these ancient writers *knew*? How did they get to such sophisticated conclusions? The only reasonable answer is that they thought it out in their heads without apparatus or mathematics.

[1] L. Le Shan, *The Medium, The Mystic and the Physicist*, Turnstone Books, London, 1974

Fig. 71
Fritjof Capra is a theoretical physicist at the University of California, Berkeley, who has written extensively on the connection between mystics' views of the world and the view suggested by modern physics.

Some of the answers which stem from this question are explored in a book which I hold to be one of the most innovative in the field of physics and philosophy to be published in recent years. [2] The author is Fritjof Capra, a physicist who now works for the Lawrence Berkeley Laboratories in the University of California. His book is an exacting and attractively orchestrated account of the similarities between the thinking of the ancient mystics and current particle physicists. In it he gives ample evidence to show that many of the physicists whose work I have been referring to throughout this book know perfectly well that there are similarities between the eastern mystic tradition and modern physics. Two examples he quotes are typical. The first is by J. Robert Oppenheimer, the physicist, who was closely involved with the development of the hydrogen bomb:

The general notions about understanding . . . which are illustrated by discoveries in atomic physics are not in the nature of things wholly unfamiliar, wholly unheard of, or new. Even in our own culture they have a history, and in Buddhist and Hindu thought, a more considerable and central place. What we shall find is an exemplification, an encouragement, and a refinement of old wisdom. [3]

The second is written by Niels Bohr:

For a parallel to the lesson of atomic theory we must turn to those kinds of epistemological problems [epistemology is the study of the method and organisation of knowledge] which already thinkers like the Buddha and Lao Tzu have been confronted, when trying to harmonise our position as spectators and actors in the great drama of existence. [4]

It was Heisenberg, whose Uncertainty Principle we looked at on page 96, who realised that the mixing of these two types of wisdom could be productive:

. . . in the history of human thinking, the most fruitful developments frequently take place at those points where two different lines of thought meet. These lines may have their roots in quite different parts of human culture, in different times or different cultural environments or different religious traditions; hence if they actually meet . . . so that a real interaction can take place, then one may hope that new and interesting developments may follow. [5]

[2] F. Capra, *The Tao of Physics*, Wildwood House, London, 1975; Fontana/Collins, London, 1976

[3] J. R. Oppenheimer, *Science and the Common Understanding*, Oxford University Press, 1954

[4] N. Bohr, *Atomic Theory and Human Knowledge*, John Wiley, New York, 1958

[5] Quoted in F. Capra, *The Tao of Physics* (op. cit.)

I asked Dr Capra how he saw the connection between physics and the paranormal as a physicist:

FC: It may be that there is a lesson in the experience of physicists for parapsychologists. What happened in physics was that they discovered a complementarity between classical concepts.

$A + B$

For instance, an electron could be a particle or a wave, but it was not a particle and a wave at the same time. And in the beginning they used to say that on Mondays and Tuesdays electrons are particles, on Wednesdays and Thursdays they're waves, and they didn't know how and why. After a while they understood that results depended on the framework of the experiment [see page 90] and there was a dynamism between those two pictures, the particle picture and wave picture. What complementarity means is that these two pictures, the particle picture and the wave picture are complementary views of one and the same reality. Both are needed, but both are mutually exclusive.

$A + B$ particle or wave

$\overline{A \cdot B}$ not (particle & wave)

$\overline{A} \cdot \overline{B} = \overline{A + B}$

KP: In that case do you think that there's a similar complementarity appearing between physics and the paranormal?

FC: That's exactly what I'm thinking. In fact, this complementarity is of a broader nature. There may be a complementarity between the manifestation of paranormal phenomena and the uses of the scientific framework to observe them, analyse them and interpret them. What I'm saying is that it may well be that *psychic phenomena may manifest themselves in full force only outside the analytic rational framework* and may diminish progressively as we become more precise in analysing them and describing them scientifically. [KP's italics.]

KP: In that case, isn't there a danger that one might fall victim to an anti-science movement in which measurement goes out of the window?

FC: Well, there is a danger of going overboard in the other direction, but there's always a danger in any major shift of concept. It was exactly the same in physics. It was a real emotional crisis for those people [Einstein, Bohr, Schrödinger and the other progenitors of the new physics], and what I'm suggesting for parapsychologists is that, at this stage of the game, they should be less bent on being scientific and should try more to get an intuitive grasp of the situation before developing a precise theory.

KP: If we were to see a science of this sort emerge in which intuition and consciousness played a real and functional part, how do you see that developing in the future?

FC: When we talk about consciousness and we talk about intuition, we're talking about qualities; we're not talking about quantities and we will have to formulate a science based on experience and quality. Traditionally our scientists reduce quality to quantity, to measurement, and therefore science cannot, I think, say very much at this stage that means anything about consciousness, because consciousness is essentially a qualitative experience.

KP: It seems to me that much in current physics is going beyond reductionism, and is suggesting there may be a broader whole beyond the current boundaries of physics?

FC: Where I have compared physics to mysticism I make precisely this point, and I show how there is an organic, holistic view emerging from physics which is quite close to the views of mystics of all ages and traditions.

KP: It seems now that physicists are talking in much more realistic terms about the relationship of their consciousness to the system they want to examine. It's as if they're talking about a real, functional connection between the two.

FC: That's true. The question of consciousness of the human mind and consciousness entered physics, when it was realised that the strict division between the observer and the observed, between mind and matter, could be made no longer, and that the observed in atomic physics depends very much on how we observe it, and depends very much on our whole conceptual framework, so that the patterns of matter that we see in physics are, as I like to put it, reflections of patterns of mind.

So you have these two realities, *patterns of matter and patterns of mind, and the two reflect one another*, you cannot say 'mind over matter', or 'matter over mind'; it's not that one causes the other, but they're mutually inter-related and reflect one another and therefore many physicists, including myself, think now that future progress in physics will be impossible unless we include the nature of consciousness explicity in our theories. But, as I said before, we will have to go far beyond the current framework of science, and a new type of science will have to enter the picture. [KP's italics.]

So here, in my view, is the 'essential' linking statement between physics and the paranormal: that *paranormal phenomena may manifest themselves in full force only outside the analytical, rational framework, that progress in physics will be impossible unless we include the nature of consciousness explicitly in our theories.*

In conversation with Fritjof Capra, I commented that these statements, taken out of context, could open the door to any number of irrational cult views of nature; in context, they are probably the essential clue to an understanding of the paranormal.

We have, by definition, to include the actions and activities of the conscious, human mind in everything we purport to study. Our enquiry has, as a first premise, to be a *participatory* enquiry. One of America's most eminent physicists, Dr John Wheeler, put it:

Nothing is more important about the quantum principle than this; that it destroys the concept of the world as 'sitting out there'. ... Measurement changes the state of the electron. The universe will never afterwards be the same. To describe what has happened, one has to cross out the old word 'observer', and put in its place the new word 'participator'. In some strange sense the universe is a participatory universe. [6]

[6] J. Wheeler, in J. Mehra Reidel (ed.), *The Physicists' Conception of Nature*, Dordrecht, Holland, 1973

After I had finished talking to the physicists who appeared in the series, I developed the strong feeling that it was the physicists who were straining at the leash to extend their view of nature, rather than the scientists working on the paranormal. It was the physicists who were looking for ways of broadening their field of enquiry, of stepping beyond the constraints of a world view which excludes consciousness as a participatory component.

Professor Geoffrey Chew is Chairman of Physics at the Lawrence Berkeley Laboratories in California; I asked him whether he thought this was true:

KP: When we look at the field of parapsychology and physics, it seems that the physicists are beginning to shift towards a view of things in which the para-psychological results are no longer outrageous. Is that a fair comment?

GC: Yes, I think that's a fair statement, and I would very much tie this with my own doubts about the absolute nature of reality. The notion that certain things are impossible is inevitably tied to an assumption that the universe is made of real things

Fig. 72
Geoffrey Chew is
Professor of Physics
and Head of
Department at the
Lawrence Berkeley
Institute in California.
He agrees that
'para-psychological
results are no longer
outrageous'.

and that things are separated in a well defined way. Once you begin to seriously question this as an absolute basis for thought, then all sorts of possibilities open up.

KP: If the physicists have moved conceptually from the point where they thought there to be an absolute reality, it's as if they could now teach parapsychologists how to do a more broadly based experiment.

GC: Well, I agree with the spirit of what you're saying but I think that could be misinterpreted. The physicists still do their experiments in the framework of absolute reality. We do not know how to formulate the notion of an experiment, except in traditional terms. What has happened is that physicists have begun to work with theories in which absolute reality is not the starting point, in which the contact with experiments is viewed as something which has to be dealt with, but which might be only an approximation to some deeper truth – let's say, which cannot be quite reached in the context of absolute reality.

KP: Of all people who are in the public eye, the physicists seem least likely to have such a broad view of the universe. Physicists are often seen by the public to be people who deal with Boyle's Law and hardware, and yet this is such a mistaken assumption. Those I've been talking to have been much more broadly based, much more philosophically inclined, much more in love with nature, much more attracted to the world about them, than I think people suppose.

GC: I think that's true. It's impossible for a person to study the great discoveries of the twentieth century in relativity and quantum mechanics and not be led to this broader view. It is paradoxical that philosophers are probably less willing, on the whole, to think in these extremely broad terms than physicists are. But it's true, I have discovered, that generally speaking physicists are more willing to loosen their way of thinking.

It is the loosening of the way of thinking which is beginning to happen at the frontiers of physics; but a loosening *without* sacrifice of reason and vigour. At the moment, I find that the general mood is uncertain. The discovery of such an integral relationship between mind and matter is very shocking to everyone and I suspect it is seen somehow as a blow to our ego. No longer are we the intellectual super-heroes of the library and the laboratory, but much lower key and involuntary participants inside the fabric of a marvellously complex, dynamic and interacting universe which we no longer can be seen to drive. We can no longer ask simple, objective questions.

A Zen story makes the point. Two novice monks were watching a flag waving on a pole and fell to arguing about whether it was the flag which was waving or whether it was the wind which was waving. To resolve their dispute, they went to the Zen master and asked him which was true. He listened in polite silence then dragged both of them by the ear to the flagpole, pulled it out of the ground and struck both of them with the pole, exclaiming, 'It is your *minds* which are waving!'

Dr Lawrence Le Shan, who made such important contributions to the television series, now talks about different realities, or different modes of being. [7] The two most important to our enquiry here he calls 'the sensory reality' and 'the clairvoyant reality'. He shows that we have a choice, as do physicists with complementarity, between entirely different ways of looking at the real world about us, and so like the physicist, actually discover different aspects of reality.

[7] L. Le Shan, *Alternative Realities*, Ballantine Books, New York, 1976

In the sensory reality:
1 All valid information comes from the senses.
2 All events happen in space and time.

3 All events have a cause.
4 Causes occur before effects.
5 Objects separate in space are separate objects.
6 Events separate in time are separate events.
7 All objects and events are composed of parts and can be dealt with separately.
8 This is the only valid way to regard reality. All other ways are an illusion.

In the clairvoyant reality:
1 All objects are part of the total fabric of being.
2 The most important aspect of any object or event is that which is part of the total.
3 Boundaries, edges and borders do not exist. All things primarily are each other.
4 Division of time into past, present and future is an error and illusion.
5 Events do not happen, they are.
6 Valid information is not gained through the senses but through a knowing of the oneness of observer and observed, spectator and spectacle.
7 The senses give a false picture of reality. They show separation of objects and events in space and time.
8 This is the only valid way to regard reality. All other ways are illusion.

I have shortened, and therefore slightly re-worded, these points from the original.

The word 'mystic' often conjures up a picture of strangeness and weirdness, someone who utters broad meaningless generalities about the world and who meets others to hold occult and esoteric ceremonies to create magical worlds and happenings.

This is an image of the mystic made by a society which is aggressively materialistic and pragmatic in its aims. This society has now, as an act of deliberation, created rules which actively discourage personal growth.

Lawrence Le Shan has spent much of his life studying the similarities between the sensory or scientific tradition and the clairvoyant or mystic tradition. What he has to say helps us to understand the 'way of knowing' that the successful subject experiences while he achieves a paranormal result. I asked him about his work in this area and how he became interested in the subject:

My analysis started with how the psychics described the world at the moment they were achieving paranormal information. For the past hundred years there has been a tremendous amount of work saying how did the psychics do it, but there was no answer to how they felt and what they experienced.

After a hundred years we were no further along the path than we had been in the beginning. When serious people ask a question for a long time and don't get an answer, they're asking the wrong question. So they then work with other questions. Finally, I came to ask what was going on at the moment paranormal information was achieved. And I began to ask serious psychics like Irene Garrett about this, Rosalind Hayward, people of this calibre. They said, 'Oh the world looks quite different, things are very different at that moment,' and they began to talk about the experience. They described a way of being in the world, of looking at the world, which was quite different from ordinary everyday experience; a way in which all things flowed into each other and in which the most important aspect of things was their connection to everything and not their identity. And after I had understood what they were saying, I began to get a clear picture which moulded together into an organised metaphysical system, and then I realised that I'd heard it before.

This was the way the mystics talked about things. Every great mystic in history, whether you go to the east or the west, had said there were two ways of being in the world: the ordinary everyday way where the most important thing about something is its individuality, its uniqueness – and the 'way of the one', as they called it, where the most important thing about something was its relativeness, its part of being in the whole. And so I found that what the psychics and the mystics were saying was exactly the same thing. They both said, in their ordinary everyday way, as they walk around the world they use the ordinary, everyday, commonsense way of organising reality, but at those moments when paranormal information is achieved, they looked at the world in a different way.... And then I realised that this is what the relativity physicists were saying, that in terms of ordinary everyday life we have to look at the world in what's called the Newtonian way [see page 43] where things are separate, things are individual, and only that's important. In terms of looking at things that were very large, or whizzing by very fast, they looked at them in another way.

Perhaps the best analogy is how we get from one place to another. If we are going on a ship or an aeroplane and going a long distance, we have to take into account the fact the earth is curved and some paths are faster than others, such as the great circle route from England to the United States; but if I'm walking from one street to another I'd better assume the world is flat and go along as if it's flat. That's the commonsense way because for me at that point it is flat, and so we can have two different ways of dealing with the world which is uncontradictory.

These two ways of being can best be looked at, in my view, as a complementarity of the mind, two modes of being inside the person, which can create two ways of connecting and interacting with the world outside the mind. In an exactly similar way to the complementarity of the physicists, both are mutually exclusive, both *do* occur and neither describes the properties of the world outside but only the interaction of the mind with the outside world.

Alex Tanous was the subject of the 'out-of-body' experiments I described earlier (see page 114). I asked him how he saw the world when he experienced being 'out of body'.

KP: Alex, you seem very well adjusted to an experience that would have other people reaching for a psychiatrist. How is it you're so calm about it? What does it feel like when you do this?

AT: When I start the experiment I feel myself in a condition that most people feel, and then suddenly, in a thought form, or in a form which then gels into a solid; I find myself where I want to be, and at that moment everything disappears from my life; all the material things, although my surroundings are still there, don't exist for me. Suddenly I'm connected with everything in the universe and I'm there living in the universe, still present in myself but with the excitement of the general relationship. I find myself there; I don't want to come back.

KP: What you're saying is optimistic, isn't it?

AT: Very optimistic, because what I feel is that I'm breaking the line of darkness between life and death and that it's a transition. And that it should be a beautiful experience we should not fear; we should wait for it with great expectation and great love. And that death does not annihilate us but gives us greater consciousness of the universe.

Many of the scientists I spoke with seem also to have a far broader view of the effects of the interconnectedness that both physics and studies of the paranormal are revealing. Earlier (see page 37) I described a remote viewing experiment I took part in with Professor Elizabeth Rauscher. I asked her about her general views on the similarities between some parts of physics and the paranormal. She replied:

I think it's very optimistic. I personally think that it is something that will give us a handle on really understanding our interconnectedness with other people and with other things in the universe. And I am talking about philosophy now and not physics.

The ideas of physicists, like complementarity, are not confined by them to their experiments and their apparatus; they affect their general view of the world in a real, powerful and very human way.

There seems to me to be little doubt that physicists are moving towards a more unified view of the universe. They are reasoning out the connections between what appear to our everyday senses to be separate events and structures. It is the anatomy of these connections which may, eventually, spell out an entirely different view of the world in which we find ourselves. This is a view so different in kind from the old mechanical view of things that it would make the science of the future sound more like poetry. The poetry would be just as precisely based upon logic and reason as the best of work in the first physics. There is no reason at all why

Fig. 73
Dr Charles Tart is the experimental psychologist who carried out the trials with Miss Z.

beauty, explanation and precision cannot co-exist. One is not the antithesis of the other. Both will probably become part of a new complementarity. Just because a mathematician is able to construct a string of symbols which describes a particular pattern of behaviour in nature, there is no reason why this part of nature should not also be astonishingly beautiful at the same time.

The mechanical science of the first physics seemed to depict the universe as a majestic and terrible place, an inhuman vastness where matter, energy and radiation boiled unceasingly in a tumult of isolated creation and destruction. The second physics is extending this view. It is not denying the titanic events which we know to occur; it is saying something very important in addition: that throughout this endless web of connection, there may be evidence of an intelligent and massively ordered design.

To understand that design we have first to look into our *own* relationship with these strange and exciting developments. Professor Rauscher said: 'It will give us a handle on really understanding our inter-connectiveness with other people....' Dr Charles Tart, the psychologist who carried out the experiment on 'Miss Z' (see page 108) extended this point of view:

It's the implications of parapsychological phenomena for understanding our own nature that is so exciting. The conventional scientific view of man is that mind and consciousness are really only a way of talking about the brain, that they are absolutely identical. If that view is true, my consciousness is totally contained in my head and I have only indirect data about the world, other people, sensory impulses. There is no direct contact. That view really is tremendously isolationist. You're really locked up somewhere else for ever, and I'm here; it leads to a sense of not caring. Now, if you accept the validity of phenomena like telepathy, there is a very real sense in which you and I are one. That is, it's possible to have a very direct kind of contact, and in that case I have much more real concern for what happens to you, whether you're happy or suffering, than if you're really forever isolated from me. Those kinds of implication are very exciting. They will have effects on how we treat one another, how we view our place in the universe, how we relate to other animals, other life forms and so forth; that's what's important. The future of parapsychology will undoubtedly include learning to control the phenomena and developing practical applications, but it's the implications of it, about our view of man, that are really much more exciting to me, and will have more impact in the long run.

If science is beginning to reveal aspects of what may be a 'design' to the universe, and that the whole of the material world did not merely evolve as a random juggling of matter, energy and radiation, how is this different from saying it is all due to God?

One of the physicists I spoke to said something which was extraordinary in this context. Such is the power and influence of the public institutions of science that he made the comment privately and not for publication against his name. He said, 'What we need now is a way of thinking which is halfway between physics and a religion.'

Rather as Fritjof Capra said in his conversation with me during the television series, future advances in physics must include a study of *consciousness*. A physics which includes a study of consciousness must include a study of the mind: a study of the mind automatically includes a study of the connection between mind, consciousness and matter.

In an increasingly real way, physics is revealing that the universe *is* our mind and our mind *is* the universe, and it is also beginning to specify the extraordinary connections which follow from the statement. As physicist Sir Arthur Eddington put it: 'The stuff of the universe is mind stuff,' and Sir James Jeans echoed this view: 'The Universe looks less and less like a great machine and more and more like a great thought.'

Professor George Sudarshan, who made such interesting contributions to our series and who is Director of the Particle Theory Unit at the University of Texas physics department wrote: 'We have thus a surrealistic universe, one in which objects merge into processes and *actions become incarnated in matter*, a world in which one entity is in many configurations at the same time and the notions of separateness and individuality are merely projections of a structure which is indescribably richer.' (Author's italics.) This is taken from the text of a lecture, the title of which would simply not have been believed a mere decade ago: 'Physics as a Spiritual Discipline'. [8] George Sudarshan is Indian by birth and spends part of each year at the Department of Physics in the Indian Institute of Science at Bangalore. Having enjoyed his rich and interesting conversation, I am sure that his experience of the two cultures has enabled him to comprehend, in a profound and intuitive way, some of the similarities between the current statements of physics and the mystic tradition.

One quite usual view of scientists is that they are people who seek to explain the whole of the universe in rational terms without reference to any intelligence, design process, or god. Yet a search of the more general writing of the great scientific innovators

[8] E. C. G. Sudarshan, 'Physics as a spiritual discipline', Nehru Memorial Lecture, 1977

reveals quite the opposite. Albert Einstein, for example, wrote: '...
cosmic religious feeling is the strongest and noblest incitement to
scientific research.' Also, 'The religious feeling of the scientist
takes the form of a rapturous amazement at the harmony of natural
law which reveals an intelligence of such superiority that, compared with it, all the systematic thinking and acting of human
beings is an utterly insignificant reflection.' [9]

My own experience has been that those scientists who have
been the most imaginative and original contributors to their own
subject have always readily admitted to a fundamental belief in a
universal intelligence or god. It has always been those who looked
to science only for its most *practical* results who have denied this
possibility.

Centuries before Einstein, Leonardo da Vinci wrote:

*Let bigots talk at leisure and heed them not. The study of nature is
well-pleasing to God and is akin to prayer. Learning of the laws of
nature, we magnify the first Inventor, the Designer of the world;
and we learn to love him, for the great love of God results from
great knowledge. Who knows little loves little.*

Study of the paranormal could go in one of two directions in the
future. It could either dwindle and be tucked away as an aberrant
and rather tiresome aspect of *'technical man'* as he struts along his
aggressive path. Alternatively it could evolve into the central
building block of an entirely new view of ourselves in relation to
the natural world about us, which could turn us in a more humane
direction and radically enrich our relationships.

With the complementarity of the mind which now lies before
us, we have an absolutely free choice of which path to take.
Perhaps, in the not too distant future, what we now call 'paranormal' will be a fully accepted part of the 'normal'.

[9] A. Einstein, *The World as I See It*, Bodley Head, London, 1935

Appendix I

Do-it-Yourself Experiments

Many of the experiments in this book can be adapted for you to try out yourself. Ninety-five per cent of the content of a good experiment is asking precisely the *right* question *before* you start work, to know in full detail the unknown you want to test.

Experimentation is an exacting and often laborious process, but if well designed and carefully performed it can lead to real and original discovery. You do not have to be a scientist to be successful. So what is it you would like to make known about the paranormal and yourself or your circle of friends? Are you a 'sheep' or a 'goat'. Which of your friends are 'sheep' and which 'goats'?

The evidence is that paranormal abilities are greatly to do with conditions of positiveness, warmth and friendliness. You are most *unlikely* to get any results with your spouse if you have just had a massive row, and most *likely* to get results if you are feeling warm and relaxed towards each other.

Ganzfeld

For a Ganzfeld experiment, you need a ping-pong ball, cut it in half with a sharp pointed pair of nail-scissors, and line the cut edges (which tend to be scratchy and sharp) with cotton wool or masking tape. You can buy a red electric light bulb and put it in a table lamp with the shade taken off. Place the lamp about two feet away from the subject, who should be warm, lying down and relaxed. Put it centrally, opposite his or her nose, so that both eyes receive about the same level of light.

For 'white noise', turn your radio to a point on the tuning scale where there is only static. Try and choose static which has an even 'waterfall' hiss, and not sharp, intermittent crackles and bangs. Then borrow a cassette tape-recorder and record the static. Radio static is *not* white noise, but it is a fair imitation. Then play the recorded static through your radio or hi-fi into any sort of earphones which fit snugly over the ears; adjust the volume to a level which the subject finds comfortable. Insist on a period of relaxation before the beginning of each experiment, to allow both the 'sender' and 'receiver' to wind down to the necessary level of mental quiet.

You can model your experiment on the protocol which Dr Carl Sargent uses; make sure that you score the various details of picture identification in the same way that he does.

Psychokinesis

You can also investigate psychokinesis in yourself or your friends. One of the simplest ways of seeing whether your mind can affect matter is to use a pair of ordinary dice.

First of all, you must turn the pair of dice into 'random' number generators. Here, there are at least two technical problems to be overcome. The first is that ordinary dice bought in the games department of a general store are *not* even. On most of them, the dots are marked by indentations. It follows that the number 'six' has six indentations on the 'six' face of the cube, and the number 'one' has one indentation. This may mean that the 'six' face is lighter than the 'one' face. The 'one' face may come down upwards less often, because it will be heavier and tend to sink to the table in the final moments of the roll of the dice. You cannot easily change the dice to allow for this, so must instead ensure that all the numbers on the dice are 'wished for' by your subjects evenly.

Further, a particular person may develop a regularity of throw, so that he tends to throw a particular number more often because of a consistent sequence of movements of his arm or wrist. To minimise this possibility, have more than one person throw the dice, or stick projections, say of balsa wood, at irregular places on the inside of your dice cup. Use an old yoghurt container as the cup. This will have the effect of bumping and turning the dice in a more irregular way while it is still being shaken in the dice cup.

Telepathy

If you would like to see whether your group can 'send' pictures, you can use a pack of cards specially designed for this purpose. You can buy what are called 'Zener' cards from the Society for Psychical Research, 1 Adam and Eve Mews, Kensington, London W8 6UG. Zener cards are in decks of 5 and have 5 different symbols: cross, circle, square, star, and wavy lines. There are 5 cards of each design in each pack.

After one run of trying to guess all 25, a subject should get 5 'hits' by chance. Supposing you were going to set 20 to 1 as the level at which an explanation other than chance must be sought for in a run or series of runs with the Zener cards, then the scores you would need for significance would be those given in the table on page 57.

If you would like to save yourself the trouble of marking out score sheets, these too can be obtained from the Society for Psychical Research in packets of 20. The same Society also sells pre-recorded cassettes containing lectures about the paranormal.

Many people hold the view that children can sometimes use paranormal abilities more readily than adults. But children enjoy encouragement and above all *reward*. Nothing bores a child more than being asked to carry out some button-pressing or card-guessing task which they find absolutely meaningless. So work with sweets and bribery. Buy a bag of boiled sweets, of similar size and shape but of two colours only. Put the same number of each colour into a box with a lid and shake them. Then put the box behind your back, take the lid off and without looking, feel for a sweet, hold it in your hand and bring your hand round and ask the child which of the two coloured sweets you are holding. If you want to extend the experiment, you can use 5 different colours of sweet and have a total of 25 sweets so that the odds are the same as those for the Zener cards.

If you prefer, you can work with two colours again, but pick up two sweets, one in each hand, and hold both hands out to your child subject and ask which hand holds say, 'the red one'. This is effectively the same as coin-tossing, and subject to the same odds assessment.

The basis of working with sweets is that you can say to your subject: 'Every one you guess right, you can keep.' Watch out though: some kids, once they find they are on to a good thing (a growing pile of free sweets), may try to fiddle the results outrageously.

Remote viewing

If you want to try remote viewing, stick to the same sort of protocol used by Drs Targ and Puthoff, but use *independent* judges to make the comparisons between the reports of the outbound group and the descriptions made by the subject at base. Try to build into your protocol as many independent observers as possible, to strengthen any claim to a 'hit' that you may subsequently make.

Metal bending

Metal bending is certainly the most experimentally fraught area in the whole paranormal field. It is quite exceptionally difficult to set up conditions which would satisfy a 'goat' investigator. People I have spoken to who have actually carried out experiments all say that some very ordinary people are quite capable of conscious or unconscious manipulation. It is an ordinary human weakness to want to be successful, and unless you can be absolutely sure that the conditions I laid down in the book can be reproduced in some equivalent form, this is probably an area to avoid. In general, try and create conditions where the *entire, recent and continuous history* of the metal is known right up to the time when the metal enters the experimental arena. During the actual experiment, the metal must be under the *continuous* view of at least two independent observers. Above all, do not trust *yourself* as observer. Remember the old lady and the professor I wrote about. Both were probably sincere and honest people, and yet their ability to observe accurately was totally faulty.

Unconscious bias

I learned this lesson, not to trust myself, in research in a particularly traumatic way. A technician and I were watching the progress of two columns of fluid in glass tubes set against scales. He watched one, I watched the other. It was a boring experiment, and we measured off fluid levels at regular intervals using stop watches. The rate of progress of each was about the same. For no particular reason, we decided to swop positions, and to my utter and total dismay, the readings started to differ by as much as 20 per cent. The upshot was that I was unconsciously moving my head in one direction to make the fluid level appear to move more quickly.

My whole attitude to research had always been to discover unknowns in as truthful a way as possible, but here was I unconsciously biasing the results in a particular direction. I was so shattered by this personal discovery that I almost gave up research altogether. However, I suppose that in the long run it sharpened my self-knowledge and improved the value of my research, and I have told the story to warn you against accepting your own observations as being the only source of accuracy.

Computers

The most unbiased 'experimenter' to be found is a machine. Many schools and colleges now have access to a mini-computer. A programme can be written to 'interrogate' a subject for e.s.p. abilities.

The programme below will perform this experiment: the computer effectively says the following:

I am going to select a number between 0 and 10 from a random source of numbers. I will then hold the number secretly until you, the subject, predict which number I have chosen. I will then compare your prediction with my random choice. If you are correct I will register 'correct'. If you are wrong I will register 'wrong'. At the end of a run I will tot up your 'corrects' and 'wrongs' and print out your score.

Here is the actual programme in BASIC language. It was written and developed by Justin Pedler, my youngest son. We have tried it, and it works reliably.

```
 10 – E = O
 20 – PRINT $ 12
 30 – PRINT 'HOW MANY GUESSES DO YOU WANT'
 40 – INPUT A
 50 – FOR C = 1 TO A
 60 – B = ABSRND % (10)
 70 – PRINT $ 12
 80 – PRINT 'MAKE GUESS BETWEEN 1 & 9'
 90 – INPUT D
100 – IF D = A GO TO 130
110 – PRINT 'WRONG'
120 – GO TO 150
130 – PRINT 'CORRECT'
140 – E = E + 1
```

```
150 – NEXT C
160 – PRINT $ 12
170 – PRINT 'YOU'VE SCORED "E" – OUT OF "A"'
180 – F = 100/A × E
190 – PRINT 'THAT IS "F" %'
200 – END
```

Explanations

Lines 20, 70, 160   Clear the screen (this instruction may vary on different machines).

30, 40   Inputs the number of times computer goes round loop (50 to 150), hence the number of guesses.

50 to 150   This is a 'For-next' loop. The computer goes around loop adding 1 to C each time it reaches line 150, until C = A.

60   Develops random number between 1 and 9. ABSRND calls up the random-number-generating subroutine.

100 to 140   Checks if value of D equals value of B. If it does, it prints 'correct' and adds 1 to E. If not, it prints 'wrong'.

190   Calculates percentage.

The apostrophe at end of Lines 80, 110, 130, is necessary to start the machine printing on a new line.

This programme can be used in a number of different ways. For example, you could test precognition or psychokinesis in much the same way as Dr Helmudt Schmidt did with his machines.

Positive results

There is no question that every so often a 'star' subject emerges (in the field of the paranormal). So what should you do if you discover a friend or relation who is especially gifted and who produces a regular stream of highly positive results?

Above all, do not try to create a sensation about it; instead contact one of the people in the list below and ask to be put in touch with an investigator who is researching the area in which your 'star' performs best. Remember the 'boredom effect' here, and do not exhaust their talent by repeated demonstration before you make contact.

Appendix II

Contacts

If you would like further advice on experiments, or on what to do with gifted subjects, people at the following addresses will help. The list is reprinted by kind permission of the Education Department of the American Society for Psychical Research, 5 West 73rd Street, New York NY 10023.

United Kingdom

Edinburgh	Dr John Beloff, Psychology Department, Edinburgh University, 60 Pleasance, Edinburgh EH8 9TJ
Nottingham	Dr Alan Gauld will help answer enquiries about graduate parapsychology study in Britain: Psychology Department, Nottingham University, University Park, Nottingham NG 2RD
Bath	Dr H. M. Collins, School of Humanities and Social Science, University of Bath, Claverton Down, Bath BA2 7AY
London	Anita Gregory, Department of Teaching Studies, Polytechnic of North London, Prince of Wales Road, London NW5 3LB
London	Professor Arthur Ellison, Department of Electrical Engineering, City University, London EC1V 4PB
Guildford	Professor S. C. Thakur, Philosophy Department, or Sue Blackmore, Psychology Department, University of Surrey, Guildford GU2 5XH

United States

New York City	Education Department, American Society For Psychical Research
New York City	Parapsychology Foundation, 29 West 57th Street, New York NY 10019

New York City   Dr Gertrude Schmeidler,
                c/o CCNY, 138th Street and Convent Avenue,
                New York NY 10031

Princeton,   Psychophysical Research Laboratories,
New Jersey   Princeton-Forrestal Center, Princeton, New Jersey

Durham,   Foundation for Research on the Nature of Man,
North Carolina Institute for Parapsychology,
                Box 6847, College Station, Durham NC 27708

Durham,   Psychical Research Foundation,
North Carolina Duke Station, Durham, NC 27706

California   Dr Charles Tart,
                Psychology Department,
                University of California,
                Davis, CA 95616

The contacts in America are far more numerous than this: for a full list,
obtain the ASPR list from the address above.

Germany

Freiburg   Dr Hans Bender,
                Institut für Grenzegebiete der Psychologie und
                Psychohygiene,
                Universität Freiburg, Freiburg im Breisgau, Eichald 12,
                West Germany

Netherlands

Utrecht   Dr Martin Johnson,
                Parapsychology Laboratory, Universiteit van Utrecht
                Varkenmarkt 2, Utrecht 2501

Australia

Tasmania   Dr H. H. J. Keil,
                University of Tasmania, Box 252C GPO,
                Hobart, Tasmania 7001

Canada

British   Dr Wayne Poley,
Columbia   Social Sciences, Douglas College,
                9260 140th Street, Surrey, BC

Toronto   Dr H. Eisenberg,
                600 Sherborne,
                Suite 609,
                Toronto, Ontario M4X 1L5

Appendix III

Further Reading

This list is alphabetical by author, and includes the books (but not journal articles) listed in the references. Titles marked * are additional to the works cited.

Andrade, E. N. da C., *An Approach to Modern Physics*, Doubleday, New York, 1957

Black, S., *Mind and Body*, William Kimber, London, 1969

Bohm, David, *Wholeness and the Implicate Order*, Routledge and Kegan Paul, London, 1980

Bohr, Niels, *Atomic Theory and Human Knowledge*, John Wiley, New York, 1958

Bohr, Niels, *Atomic Physics and the Description of Nature*, Cambridge University Press, 1934

Bowles, N., Hynds, F. and Maxwell, J., *Psi Search*, Harper and Row, New York, 1978

Campbell, J., *The Masks of God*, Condor Books, London, 1976

Capra, Fritjof, *The Tao of Physics*, Wildwood House, London 1975; Fontana/Collins, London, 1980

* de Reincourt, Amaury, *The Eye of Shiva*, Souvenir Press, London, 1980

* Ebon, Martin, *Test Your ESP*, New American Library, New York, 1970

Einstein, Albert, *Relativity*, Crown Publishers, New York, 1927

Einstein, Albert, *The World as I See It*, Bodley Head, London, 1935

Einstein, Albert, *Autobiographical Notes*, Harper and Row, New York, 1949

Frisch, Otto, *The Nature of Matter*, Thames and Hudson, London, 1972

Garrett, E., *Awareness*, Creative Age Press, New York, 1943

* Gauld, Alan and Cornell, A., *Poltergeists*, Routledge and Kegan Paul, London, 1979

Green, Celia, *Out-of-body Experiences*, Hamish Hamilton, London, 1968

* Grof, Stanislav, *Realms of the Human Unconscious*, Du Hon, New York, 1976

Hansel, C. E. M., *ESP: a Scientific Evaluation*, Scribner, New York, 1966

Hasted, J. B., *The Metal-benders*, Routledge and Kegan Paul, London, 1981

Heisenberg, W., *Across the Frontiers*, Harper and Row, New York, 1974

* Inglis, Brian, *Natural and Supernatural: a History of the Paranormal*, Hodder and Stoughton, London, 1977

* Inglis, Brian, *Natural Medicine*, Collins, London, 1979

Josephson, Brian, *The Iceland Papers*, Essentia Research Associates, Wisconsin, 1979

* Koestler, Arthur, *The Roots of Coincidence*, Hutchinson, London, 1971; Picador, London, 1972

* Kupiner, Stanley and Rubin, Daniel, *The Energies of Consciousness*, Interface, New York, 1975

Le Shan, Lawrence, *The Medium, the Mystic and the Physicist*, Turnstone Books, London, 1974

Le Shan, Lawrence, *Alternative Realities*, Ballantine Books, New York, 1976

Lorens, A., Einstein, A., Minkowski, H. and Weyle, H., *Principles of Relativity*, Dover, New York, 1952

Mackenzie, A., *Riddle of the Future*, Arthur Barker, London, 1974

* Mishlove, Jeffrey, *The Roots of Consciousness*, Random House, New York, 1975

Oppenheimer, J. R., *Science and the Common Understanding*, Oxford University Press, 1954

* Orme-Johnson, D. and Farrow, J. T. (eds.), *Collected Research Papers on Transcendental Meditation Program*, Maharishi European Research University Press, 1979

Owen, I. and Sparrow, M., *Conjuring Up Philip*, Harper and Row, New York, 1976

Pedler, Kit, *The Quest for Gaia*, Souvenir Press, London, 1979; Granada, London, 1981

Randall, John, *Parapsychology and the Nature of Life*, Abacus, London, 1977

* Randall, John, *Tests for Extrasensory Perception*, Society for Psychical Research, London

Reidel, J. Mehra (ed.), *The Physicists' Conception of Nature*, Dordrecht, Holland, 1973

* Roll, W., *The Poltergeist*, Scarecrow Press, Metuchen, New Jersey, 1976

Rosenthal, M., *Experimenter Effects in Behavioural Research*, Appleton-Century-Crofts, New York, 1966

Rozenthal, S. (ed.), *Niels Bohr*, North Holland Publishing, Amsterdam, 1967

* Samuels, Mike and Nancy, *Seeing with the Mind's Eye*, Random House, New York, 1975

Schatzman, M., *The Story of Ruth*, Duckworth, London, 1980

Schmeidler, Gertrude and McConnell, R., *ESP and Personality Patterns*, Yale University Press, 1958

Schrödinger, Erwin, *What is Life and Mind and Matter?*, Cambridge University Press, 1955

Smith, J. M., *The Dimensions of Healing*, Academy of Parapsychology and Medicine, 1972

Tanous, Alex, *Beyond Coincidence: One Man's Experience with Psychic Phenomena*, Doubleday, New York, 1976

Targ, Russell and Puthoff, Harold, *Mind-Reach*, Delacorte, New York, 1977; Jonathan Cape, London, 1977

Tart, Charles, *Psi*, E. P. Dutton, New York, 1977

Tart, Charles, Puthoff, Harold and Targ, Russell (eds.), *Mind at Large*, Praeger Scientific, New York, 1979

* Underwood, Peter, *Dictionary of the Occult and Supernatural*, Fontana, London, 1979

Watts, Alan, *Does it Matter?*, Vantage Books (Random House), New York, 1971

* Wilber, Ken, *The Spectrum of Consciousness*, Quest Books, Theosophical Publishing House, Wheaton, Illinois; London, 1977

Zukav, Gary, *The Dancing Wu Li Masters*, Rider Hutchinson, London, 1979; Fontana/Collins, London, 1980

A selected bibliography in Parapsychology for Students and Instructors, twenty-seven pages long, is available from the American Society for Psychical Research, 5 West 73rd Street, New York, NY 10023.

Appendix IV   *Who Believes it?*

Brian Inglis on answers to The Times

The controversial an

Eight years ago the late Dr Christopher Evans composed a questionnaire on parapsychology for the *New Scientist*; and what he wrote about its aims will serve also for the questionnaire in *The Times* last October. It was not designed, he explained, to show what readers in general believed, because the sample was necessarily self-selecting, " being composed only of those who, 1, are basically interested in the topic anyway; 2, feel pretty strongly about it one way or the other; and 3, have the time and energy to find an envelope and stamp and actually mail the thing off ".

But at least, he felt, the answers would give some idea of how those readers looked upon " this controversial and problematical field ".

The results surprised the deeply sceptical Dr Evans; and

they are worth recalling, as they provided the first indication that scientists' century-old scepticism was on the wane. It was an unusually large sample and, so far as could be judged, reasonably representative. Yet 25 per cent, replying to the first question, held extra-sensory perception to be an established fact, and a further 42 per cent held it to be a likely possibility. Only 3 per cent held it to be an impossibility.

A poll of academics in the United States has since shown how far scepticism there, too, has been eroded. Of more than 2,000 people holding positions in universities, half replied; and of those who were involved in the sciences, 9 per cent thought ESP an established fact and 45 per cent a likely possibility.

Academics in general put the proportions at 16 per cent, an

established fact; 50 per cent, a likely possibility. And the proportions would have been decidedly more favourable had psychologists been omitted: it was the " hard " scientists, notably the physicists, who were most in favour.

This may persuade those readers — a tiny proportion — who have complained that *The Times* was making itself look ridiculous by running such a questionnaire. After the best part of a century when no scientific journal would consider a paper giving the results of trials of ESP or psychokinesis (except if they were negative, or revealed fraud), they are at last being accepted.

Even so, one of the surprises from this questionnaire is the high proportion of the samples who have become acquainted with psychic phenomena through the literature of scientific studies. Extensive though

that literature now is, little of it has been allowed to appear in journals like *Nature* or *Science*.

The chief value of the questionnaire, to my mind, is that it provides a kind of league table to what people who are interested in the subject are prepared to accept. Unluckily we do not have an equivalent for most of the questions from —say—1970, to judge how opinions have changed; but some phenomena have surely come up in the world. Ten years ago, I suspect, few readers would even have heard of " out of the body experiences "; now, more than half the sample believe them to exist, a slightly higher proportion than believe haunting to exist (though admittedly " haunting " is a loose term, which may have caused some confusion).

Reincarnation, too, has surely

	Total
	1,314

Q 1. Unusual experiences do not always have a ready scientific or natural explanation at the present level of knowledge. Do you believe that psychic experiences

	%
Certainly exist	64
Probably exist	17
Possibly exist	17
Certainly do not exist	2
Not answered (N/A)	—

Q 2. For those who believe that they do, here is a list of the major psychic phenomena reported. Would you say whether you believe the following exist or not?

ESP	Yes	83
	No	6
	N/A	11
Telepathy	Yes	83
	No	7
	N/A	10
Contact with the dead	Yes	38
	No	38
	N/A	24
Apparitions of the living	Yes	33
	No	37
	N/A	30
Out of body experiences	Yes	54
	No	23
	N/A	23
Reincarnation	Yes	29
	No	44
	N/A	27
Haunting	Yes	53
	No	25
	N/A	22
Poltergeists	Yes	52
	No	25
	N/A	23
Dowsing	Yes	70
	No	12
	N/A	18

Q 3. Which of the following sources of information acquainted you with ESP or other psychic phenomena?

- Newspaper and magazine articles, media, popular books — 52
- Personal experiences of your own — 66
- Experiences of persons you know — 54
- Literature from scientific studies of the paranormal — 36
- Lectures on the subject — 9

- No acquaintance so far — 3
  - N/A — 1

Q 4. In your opinion, is extra sensory perception (ESP)

An establiished fact	51
A likely possibility	33
A remote possibility	11
An impossibility	3
Don't know	1
N/A	1

Q 5. Do you believe in pre-cognition, that is, experiencing knowledge of something that has not yet happened?

Yes	73
No	19
N/A	8

Q 6. Have you had any previous experience?

Yes	51
No	42
N/A	7

Q 7. Have you ever had a dream that came true concerning events which you did not know about, or expect before the dream?

Once	15
More than once	27
Never	53
N/A	5

Q 8. If you have had an ESP dream, did the real life event happen?

As you were dreaming	6
Before your dream	5
After your dream	36
N/A	5

Q 8A. Was the dream about?

Daily happenings	24
Disasters	9
Death	11
Other	8
N/A	5

Q 9. Have you ever had, while awake impression, haunches or visions concerning events you did not know about or expect, but which turned out to be true?

Once	9
More than once	47
Never	39
N/A	5

Q 10. Did the events happen?

At the time of your impressions	20

How readers

Before your impressions	8
After your impressions	41
N/A	4

Q 11. Were your impressions about?

Daily happenings	38
Disasters	11
Death	14
Other	11

Q 12. How did you experience it?

Saw	9
Heard	6
Felt	18
Just knew	40
Other	4
N/A	3

Q 13. Have you ever experienced telepathy that is awareness of what is going on in another person's mind—when you had no normal means of knowing and verified it with that person afterwards?

Occasionally	34
Frequently	24
Never	35
N/A	7

Q 14. Have you had any contact with someone who has died?

Once	10
More than once	19
Never	66

Q 15. If it happened, how did you experience it?

Saw	10
Heard voice	9
Heard noise of movements	4
Was touched	4
Felt presence only	15
Other	6
N/A	5

Q 16. Was anyone else with you and in a position to observe?

Yes	11
No	17
Who	1
N/A	6

DECEMBER 20 1980

questionnaire on the paranormal

the problematical

been given a boost by the recent television publicity for regression to "past lives" under hypnosis. I doubt whether it would have mustered even 10 per cent before.

It should be stressed that the questionnaire came into being not simply to provide a base, as it were, for future comparisons here of this kind. Much of it was devised by Dr Karlis Osis, in the United States, in collaboration with Dr Erlunder Haraldsson of the University of Iceland; the intention being to use it in countries all over the world, to find what differences there are—and what similarities.

There were, however, some additions to the Osis-Haraldsson list, including dowsing. The fact it was included riled L. J. Latham, vice-president of the British Society of dowsers, who claimed in a letter that dowsers were "appalled" at their inclu-

sion. He would probably have been even more irritated at the reason dowsing is commonly ignored by United States parapsychologists: they assume that "water-witching", as it is called there, is bogus.

Clearly it is not regarded as bogus here. I suspect that it would get a high vote in its favour even among people who are not interested in the subject. But Mr Latham's complaint was unjustified. The question that was asked in the questionnaire was about experiences which "do not always have a ready scientific or natural explanation at the present level of knowledge"—this being, in fact, the definition of paranormal phenomena. If Mr Latham has a scientific explanation for dowsing, it will come as a surprise to most members of his organization—and, I would guess, as a Nobel Prize for whoever has provided it.

There was another purpose behind the questionnaire: to enable people who have had strange, unaccountable and sometimes deeply disturbing experiences to describe them, and to say whether they would like further investigation.

Outright scepticism has become a rarity, but many people now take the "so what!" line: perhaps the paranormal exists, but does it matter? To those who experience it, it clearly often matters a great deal. Many of them would welcome advice and reassurance of a kind they clearly have not had.

Several of the letters attached to returned questionnaires tell of hallucinatory experiences, poltergeist-type manifestations, or disembodied voices. As they appear to be from eminently sensible people, naturally puzzled or disturbed by their experiences, it is absurd to try

to explain them away in stock sceptics fashion as a compound of lies, distortions and incipient insanity.

Other letters tell a different story: of the potential value of readers' experiences, such as hearing warnings of impending danger when driving a car—the "sixth sense" in operation.

Socrates used to go into trances, the better to listen to the voice of his "daemon"; it would frequently interrupt to check him, he told his judges at his trial, when he was going to make some mistake. This, surely, is a faculty worth exploring; not just treating as a psychiatric condition.

Following up the letters will take time; but it should help to a better understanding of this still inadequately explored territory, so that better advice and help can be given in future to those who are in need of them.

answered

Q 17. Was a pet with you at the time?
Yes   6
No   21
N/A   6

Q 18. Did it show any sign of stress or unusual behaviour?
Yes   4
No   9
Don't know   10

Q 19. Have you ever seen or heard while you were awake someone who you were later able to ascertain was elsewhere at the time?
Once   7
More than once   5
Never   81
N/A   7

Q 20. It happened, how did you experience it?
Saw   7
Heard voice   4
Heard noise of movements   1
Was touched   1
Felt presence only   3
Other   1
N/A   6

Q 21. Was anyone else with you and in a position to observe?
Yes   3
No   8
If yes, who   *
N/A   6

Q 22. Was something special happening to that person at that time?
Yes   4
No   6
Description   1
N/A   6

Q 23. Was a pet with you at the time?
Yes   2
No   9
N/A   6

Q 24. Did it show any sign of distress or unusual behaviour?
Yes   1
No   4
N/A   8

Q 25. Have you ever felt, while awake and not dreaming, that your consciousness was outside of your physical body so that you perceived your environment from a point away from your physical location?
Once   12
More than once   18
Induced at will   6
Never   59
N/A   6

Q 26. Have you ever had any experience which has convinced you that you must have had a previous life, or lives?
Once   5
More than once   11
Never   76
N/A   7

Q 27. While awake, have you had the impression that you are witnessing some scene or event in the past?
Once   4
More than once   16
Never   64
N/A   8

Q 28. Do you believe in haunting?
Yes   52
No   21
Don't know   23
N/A   4

Q 29. Have you ever lived in or visited a house in which you personally experienced haunting phenomena?
Once   16
More than once   19
Never   57
N/A   4

Q 30. If yes, how did you experience it?
Saw   11
Heard voice   5
Heard noise of movements   14
Was touched   3
Felt presence only   17
Other   4
N/A   6

Q 31. Has anyone else observed it?
Yes   27

No   6
Don't know   4
N/A   14

Q 32. Have you ever observed an object being moved, disturbed or bent without any apparent physical cause?
Once   6
More than once   8
Never   78
N/A   8

Q 33. If you have, were these movements associated with any particular person?
A living person   5
A dead person   4
No   5
N/A

Q 34. Were these disturbances also observed by somebody else?
Yes   11
No   2
Whom   1
N/A   —

Q 35. At the time, were there any children in the house?
Yes   6
No   7
N/A

Q 36. Have you ever tried to "dowse" to find either water, oil, minerals or some hidden object with the aid of a forked hazel twig, pendulum or other object?
Once   14
More than once   25
Never   57
N/A   4

Q 37. If you have, did you feel the dowsing reaction such as a "Twitch" of the twig?
Once   5
More than once   18
Never   14
N/A   2

Q 38. Have you participated in, or witnessed, successful dousing in circumstances which have convinced you that the faculty is genuine?
Once   14
More than once   25
Never   44
N/A   17

Index

Figures in italics refer to illustration captions.